The Donegal Highlands.

Anonymous

The Donegal Highlands.
Anonymous
British Library, Historical Print Editions
British Library
1866]
8°.
10390.c.8.

10390. c 8

THE DONEGAL HIGHLANDS.

.

THE

DONEGAL HIGHLANDS.

"How divine,
The liberty for frail, for mortal, man
To roam at large among unpeopled glens
And mountainous retirements, only trod
By devious footsteps ; regions consecrate
To oldest time !"

WORDSWORTH'S *Excursion.*

DUBLIN:

A. MURRAY & CO., 40 FLEET STREET,
WESTMORELAND STREET.

LONDON, OXFORD, AND CAMBRIDGE:
RIVINGTONS.

CONTENTS.

CONTENTS.

INTRODUCTION.

WITHIN the past year or two, some of the most eloquent pens in Great Britain have written of Irish scenery in a strain of the highest eulogy. It has been urged as a reproach to Englishmen, (and, we may add, Irishmen,) who can afford to travel, that they are given to tedious and expensive tours abroad, while within a few days' journey of home, they leave unvisited scenery incomparably finer than much of what they go so far to see. Happily, the old caricature depicting Ireland as a land where nothing is to be seen but fighting, drinking, and superstition, has been taken down from its high place, and it is no small satisfaction that the first of English journals has of late repeatedly recommended our island as one of the most desirable places in the world in which to spend a holiday with pleasure and profit. And already has the spread of correct information regarding Ireland borne fruit. The number of Englishmen visiting our shores increases day by day, and there is reason to hope that the increasing intercourse, by making this country and its people better known, will lead to a wider diffusion of kindly feeling between the two nations, and to other results beneficial to both, especially to our own.

Apart from the interest—and it is deep and manifold—which he feels in the subject itself, these considerations constitute a motive strong enough to make the writer of the following pages desire to bring under the notice of the public a district which possesses as many attractions for the tourist as any part of the United Kingdom. Donegal is unsurpassed in beauty of mountain, lake, and glen; its coast offers some of the finest cliff scenery in the world. What has been said a few weeks back of Ireland in the London *Times* is especially applicable to this district :—" Ireland, with her vast uncultivated tracts, her wild mountains, her broad lakes, her teeming rivers, is just the place for a keen sportsman, who wishes for a few weeks of healthy exercise to indemnify him for the confinement of a town life." * Donegal possesses, too, innumerable sources of interest for the antiquary, the geologist, and the botanist; and yet, with all its attractions, it is a *terra incognita* to the generality of tourists, although within one hour's rail of Derry, while it may be reached in eight hours from Dublin, and in about half that time from Belfast.

Geographically, the county of Donegal is a peninsula at the extreme north-west of Ireland. A straight line drawn from the estuary of the Erne to the estuary of the Foyle would roughly indicate its boundary on the south-eastern side; on every other side it is bounded by the sea. The clearest idea of the physical conformation of the county may be gained by fixing on a chain of mountains, beginning from the south near Lough Derg, and running northward with a slight deflection to the west to Bloody Foreland, as forming a backbone to the county. In this line occur the highest elevations and the deepest passes in the whole of the Highland district, the highest points being Barnesmore (1491 feet;) Bluestack (2219 feet;) Aghla

* *Times*, October 10, 1865.

1953 feet;) Slieve Snaght (2240 feet;) and Errigal (2466 feet.) Starting from Lough Derg, we soon meet with the Gap of Barnesmore, a deep pass running right through the mountain from south-west to north-east, the sides of which rise on either side like a wall to the height of over a thousand feet. At the eastern extremity of the Gap is Lough Mourne, the source of the Mourne Beg, which, after a circuitous route, makes its way eventually into the Foyle. The waters descending from the mountains that flank the western extremity are gathered into Lough Esk, from which a river of the same name flows down to the sea at Donegal. Somewhat to the north of the Gap of Barnesmore are the Croaghgorm, or Bluestack mountains, a noble group drained on the east by the Reelan river, which discharges its waters into the Finn, and on the west by the Eanymore and Eanybeg, which empty themselves into the sea at Inver. Here a great arm is given off to the west, which, after forming the Binbane range, runs out into the ocean, passing into a peninsula terminating in the magnificent precipices of Slieve League and Slievatooey. Following the main chain farther to the north, we find it again cut through by a deep pass running in a direction parallel to the Gap of Barnesmore. In this valley is Lough Finn, over whose dark waters Aghla rises precipitously, (1500 feet.) The river Finn issues from the eastern extremity of the lake, and after draining an extensive highland district on its way to Stranorlar, flows eastward to Lifford, where, joined by the Mourne, it spreads out into the Foyle, and flows thence in majestic stream to Derry. The drainage of the western side of Aghla is done by the Stracastle and Shallagan streams, which deliver their waters into the Owenea, below Glenties, to be carried westward to the Bay of Loughrosmore. Close upon the pass of Lough Finn, and parallel to it, is another intersecting the county right across from the Gweebarra Bay to Sheephaven. Beginning at the south-west this valley comprises first the noble estuary of the Gweebarra running some seven miles up into the heart of the mountains, then a deep defile narrowing towards Lough Barra, a little above which place the Glendowan mountains and Slieve Snaght almost meet at the point where the watershed is attained. Here begins the deep Glen Veagh, which, after emerging from between the Derryveagh and Dooish ranges, opens out into the

valley of the Owencarrow, and keeping still in its
north-east course, declines from Glen Lough to the
sea. The Glendowan mountains go off in a south-
eastern direction from the Derryveagh range, making at the angle a basin in which repose the waters
of the beautiful Gartan Lough, and then falling
gradually to the south and east form a plateau
which is drained by the Lannan and the Swilly,
both which rivers flow into Lough Swilly—the
former at Rathmelton, the latter at Letterkenny.
From the Derryveagh mountains a branch is given
off to the north-east, passing into Lough Salt (1546
feet) mountain, between Kilmacrenan and Carrigart, the Knockalla Hills (1194 feet) in Fanad,
and Slieve Snaght (2019 feet) in Inishowen. The
elevated sea-board thus raised on the north is
cloven through in three places, the indentations
forming Mulroy Bay, Lough Swilly, and Lough
Foyle. To return to the main chain: north of the
great pass of the Gweebarra and Glen Veagh is
another intersection running like the others from
south-west to north-east, between the northern side
of Slieve Snaght and Errigal. The valley on the
eastern side is drained by the Culabber, north of
which are Aghla-mor, Aghla-beg, and Muckish,

(2197 feet,) which, falling towards the north, breaks off abruptly in the magnificent precipices of Horn Head. Towards the west are Dunlewy Lough and Lough Nacung, guarded by the beautiful mountain of Errigal and a mountain ridge that stretches out to the north-west, terminating in the distant Bloody Foreland.

The geology of Donegal has not yet been so thoroughly explored as that of other parts of the kingdom. Its outlines, however, are well known, and may be easily defined. Mica-slate is the formation of by far the greater portion of the surface rock, beginning at the river Erne and stretching eastward to Inishowen Head, northward into the middle of the county, and westward to the Atlantic. It not unfrequently appears in schistose formations. North of the great mica-slate field is a belt of granite of from four to fourteen miles in breadth, extending from Loughrosmore to Sheephaven, thus traversing the county from south-west to north-east. It appears also in narrow belts between Sheephaven and Lough Swilly. It occasionally passes into gneiss, and is for the most part coarsely granular and of a reddish-brown colour, imparting a brownish tincture to the streams that carry down its *débris*. Quartz rock forms nearly the whole of the sea-board outside this granite field, and runs somewhat inland in a broad belt across Lough Swilly and out to Malin Head, at the extreme north of Inishowen. A belt of carboniferous limestone, about six miles in mean breadth, of the same kind as the great limestone field of central Ireland, curves round the western coast from the southern boundary of the county to Bruckless, near Killybegs. Primitive limestone also occurs in patches in very many places in the mica-slate field, and around the quartz formation. Besides the carboniferous and primitive, the magnesian, marly, and other varieties of limestone occur in considerable quantities. Veins of crystallized trap are found in the quartz rocks on the northern coast, and in sparse nodules in the mica-slate, the granite, and the primitive limestone. Porphyritic formations are likewise met with. At Dunlewy, near the Errigal mountain, there is a bed of white marble, so fine-grained as to be adapted to the most delicate operations of the chisel; it closely resembles the Parian marble. Besides this, other beautiful marbles, particularly the dove and rose-coloured, may be obtained from this county.

Donegal, it is said, is richer in mineral wealth than any other district in Ireland. Besides its marbles, it possesses rare and useful clays, viz., pipeclay, potters' clay, porcelain clay, iron ochre, iron and copper pyrites, and lead ore in great abundance. Yet, though so promising a field for mining speculation, it has not been fortunate enough to attract the mining capitalist to its borders. Mines have, indeed, been opened here, but in every case abandoned, chiefly, it would appear, from want of funds.

The agricultural produce of Donegal consists mainly of potatoes, oats, and flax. The proportion of unreclaimed waste to the arable land of the county is as seven to three, the soil over the mica-slate being cold and moorish, and that over the granite and quartz formations moorish also, and thin. In the district extending from Stranorlar and Letterkenny to the Foyle, where the soil is deep and rich, the farming is of the first class. The soil is warm and productive over the carbon-iferous limestone.

The manufacturing industry is confined to the making of kelp, hand-knit hosiery, and sewed muslin, all which sources afford but a very limited employment to the number of hands whose labour might be commanded.

The principal civil division of the county is into six baronies—viz., Inishowen and Raphoe, occupying the eastern half, and Kilmacrenan, Boylagh, Banagh, and Tyrhugh, the western half. The assizes are held at Lifford, and quarter-sessions at Buncrana, Donegal, Glenties, Letterkenny, and Lifford. In 1841, the population numbered 296,448, and in 1851, it fell to 255,161. Between 18,000 and 20,000 children receive primary instruction in the National Schools, which have been worked with especial success in those remote districts around Kilcar, Glenties, and Dungloe.

The following Excursions open with such an outline of the history of Donegal as exhibits in a connected whole the various disjointed historical *morceaux*, suggested by many of the places described in these pages. The utility of some such summary to the general reader is obvious. It may, however, strike the critical reader, that this plan must needs involve a deal of repetition, but though this is true to a limited extent, it will be seen, after a moment's reflection, that the necessity of repetition, which, in this case, will be rather reference than repetition, is, in truth, lessened by the introduction of a preliminary historical notice; because, in the absence of such an outline, it would be necessary to introduce many summaries, according as the places visited suggested noteworthy historic incidents or events, in order to give the reader a satisfactory idea of the facts associated with these scenes. We have heard it repeatedly said that the frequent occurrence of proper names of a harsh and difficult orthography repels the mass of our readers from the perusal of Irish history. The objection may, indeed, be reasonable in reference to a large portion of our annals. But the same objection would hold good as well in regard to the records of every nation whatever that has a history. When we remember how much of our time at school we were obliged to give to getting by heart the names of the characters in heathen mythology, and to the study of the fictions—most of them of very questionable morality—in which they figure, we ought not, one would think, to grow impatient at the names of characters who have acted a part, often a noble part, in real life. Let us hope, at least, that the names of the men and places which occur in these pages will not deter the visitor, who seeks to know as well as to see, from the perusal of the little of historical matter they offer.

Since Donegal has been more frequented, the hotel accommodation has considerably improved. All that is wanted to make it everything that could be desired is a fair share of encouragement from the landed proprietors. Speaking generally, the supply is fully equal to the demand. There are at the present moment many comfortable hotels; and if in some few places the accommodation is not all that could be wished, the visitor to Donegal will be sure to find everywhere the people civil and intelligent.

A glance at the map attached to these Excursions will enable the traveller to understand the plan of their arrangement, and at any moment to "define his position." One main route is traced through the country, touching at the most attractive scenes in the whole district, and from convenient points of this main route minor Excursions are traced to all the other places of interest.

THE DONEGAL HIGHLANDS.

DONEGAL is rich in early remains and memories of the past. The general tourist will need a summary of the history of Tyrconnell to aid him to interpret those echoes of the olden time, which he will be glad to catch in the traditions and legends of the country for their poetic if not their historic interest.

At the earliest dawn of Irish history this district comes prominently into view, shrouded, indeed, in those fabulous surroundings that dim the first beginnings of every nation tracing its origin up to a remote antiquity. Here, on a plain near Lough Swilly, was fought the battle of Magh-Ith, "the first battle fought in Ireland,"[*] between the Fomorians, a piratical tribe just then landed on the island, and the Nemedians,[†] the first inhabitants, who had settled here a short time before. The Fomorians engaged in the fight were all killed, but their tribe still remained in strength on the sea-coast, whence

---

[*] Annals of the Four Masters.
[†] The descendants of Neimhidh, pronounced Nevy.

A

they kept up a perpetual war with the Nemedians in the interior. Torry seems to have been the chief stronghold of the Fomorians. We find chronicled under the year A.M. 3066 a fierce attack on Tor-Conainn, or Conaing's Tower, in this island. The tower was taken by storm and the work of demolition completed, when, succour arriving by sea to the pirates, the battle was renewed on the strand, and the combatants closed in an obstinate struggle from which the returning tide did not make them relax till they all, with but a very few exceptions, perished together in the waves. The power of the Nemedians was completely broken in this battle, and the Fomorians now ruled the coast with undisputed sway. Two hundred years passed away, and a new colony, known as the Firbolgs, probably of the same stock originally as the Nemedians, appeared in Erinn. And many years afterwards came a strange race, the Tuatha De-Dennans, led by Nuadh of the Silver Hand,* who at once subjugated the Firbolgs, and formed an alliance with the Fomorians. Some years later the Fomorians take the field against the De-Dennans, and Nuadh is killed by " Balor of the Mighty Blows," † the leader of the Fomorians, whose principal residence is supposed to have been at Torry, from the many traditions re-

---

* *Nuadht-Airgetlamh,* in the Irish.   † Four Masters.

specting him there. Balor was himself killed in this battle by Lewy the Long-handed, (Lugh Lamhfhada,) his own daughter's son.

When Ith, the adventurous pioneer of the Milesians, sailed from Spain to seek out "the land to the west," it was in the county of Donegal, near the Laggan, on the shores of Lough Swilly, he first landed; and it was here, on the plain called Magh-Ith,* the Tuatha De-Dennans attacked him and his followers. He escaped to his ship, but not before he had received a wound which proved fatal. He was carried back dead to Spain. Then followed that second expedition to Inis Ealga,† which led to the establishment of the Milesians in the land. We pass down to the reign of Cimbaeth,‡ remarkable for the building of the famous palace of Emania, and, according to the more critical of our annalists, the starting-point of authentic chronology in Irish history. According to the accounts of the time, a prince named Aodh Ruadh, *i.e.*, Red Hugh, who had enjoyed kingly power in Ulster, was drowned at the cataract of Ballyshannon, (hence the name Easaroe,§) and his daughter Macha, a very Semiramis, having

* The precise locality has not yet been identified.
† As Ireland was then called.
‡ Pronounced Kimbahe. 661 years before Christ, according to the computation of the Four Masters.
§ Eas-Aodh-Ruadh, the Cataract of Red Hugh.

made good her claim to succeed him by force of arms, married her competitor, Cimbaeth, who thus became sole ruler in the north. Towards the end of the fourth century of the Christian era (379) reigned Niall of the Nine Hostages, one of the most famous of the Pagan kings of Ireland. Niall was the founder of the Hy-Niall, a race for many an age to come rulers in the land. Eight of his sons became the heads of princely houses. Four settled in the Meath district, and four settled in Ulster; and thus came the southern Hy-Niall and the northern Hy-Niall. Amongst the four brothers who settled in the north were Conall and Eoghan.* From Conall came the name and race of Kinel-Conall, while Eoghan was the father of the Kinel-Eoghan. Hence the districts of Tyr-Conall and Tyr-Eoghan, with their respective governing septs, O'Donnell and O'Neil—names afterwards so illustrious in the Irish annals. Conall received the appellative Gulban from Ben Gulben, the modern Benbulben of the county of Sligo, where he was fostered. That he was a man far above the common sort we may gather from the annalists, and more particularly from the traditions in which his strength and daring

---

* Pronounced, and usually written, *Owen*. The orthography of most of the proper names that figure in Irish history is marvellously various, a fact which will account for the slight variety in the spelling of a few names that occur in these pages.

have been handed down with all the exaggeration of an Ossianic tale. He was slain in an encounter with a tribe inhabiting a district in the present county of Cavan. It is recorded that Eoghan died of grief for the death of his brother, and was buried at Eskaheen, in the peninsula, which is named after him, Inishowen.

St Patrick's visit to Ireland, (432,) and the ready acceptance of the gospel by the inhabitants, and the fervour of the proselytes, form perhaps one of the brightest and most interesting chapters in the history of Christianity. Tyrconnell shared in the general blessing. There is a beautiful tradition connected with the great saint's visit to this district. The apostle in his progress through the island, after resting on " Magh-Ith, in Cinel Chonaillhe, went in his chariot the next day to the stream which is called Daol."* The spindles of the chariot broke, were mended, and broke again; and then Patrick, addressing those with him, said, through the spirit of prophecy, " Do not wonder, for the land from the stream northwards does not stand in need of a blessing, for that a son shall be born there who shall be called the Dove of the Churches, (Collum-Cille,) who shall bless the land to the north, and it is in honour of him that God has prohibited my blessing this land." Ath-an-Charpaid, (ford of the chariot,) on

* The river Deel, or Burndale.

the Daol, is the name of that ford. St Patrick also blessed the south side of the cataract (Eas) of Bally-shannon, and said that he left the north side to be blessed by Collum-Cille.*

About a century afterwards, this Dove of the Churches, having gone out from Cinel-Conall, returned to give the blessing, which, according to St Patrick, had been reserved for him. He was a youth of princely descent. His name was Crimthain. His father was Felim, the grandson of Conal-Gulban, and his mother, Ethnea, a daughter of the royal house of Cahir-Mor, of Leinster. Born in 521, he was, according to the usage of the time, placed in fosterage with a relative at Kilmacrenan. "From his boyhood he had been instructed in the love of Christ, and by the grace of God, and his zeal for wisdom, had so preserved the integrity of his body, and the purity of his soul, that though dwelling on earth he appeared to live like the saints in heaven."† He passed from his fosterage to the school of St Finian, and made a course of studies under this famous master, in the school at Moville, at the head of Strangford Lough. Thence he passed to another celebrated Finian at the famous school of Clonard, and thence through other schools; for

---

* Martyrology of Donegal—*Colum-Cille.*
† Life of St Columba, by Adamnan.

already had there risen in Erinn many institutions in which sanctity and learning were taught together. Famed throughout the length and breadth of the land for his learning, and still more for his sanctity, abundantly attested by splendid miracles, he took priest's orders, and returned to the north about the year 544. He traversed Cinel-Conall, leaving monuments of his piety and zeal on the hill of Doire Calgaigh,* on the rocks of Torry, in the remote Seanglean, everywhere, on sea-cliff and in deep glen, and, though these monuments, like all that is perishable, have yielded to the corrosive action of time, and, in but too many instances, to the more destructive fury of man, the traveller of to-day will be able from the traditions still clinging to the rude cross, or the blessed well, or the grass-grown remains of a chapel, to gather a better record of him than could have endured on inscribed stone. His blessing went beyond the lands of Tyrconnell. His wonderful sanctity of life, and his many miraculous tokens of divine favour, marked him out as indeed a man of God, and drew disciples around him. Thus he became the father of an order of monks, distinguished, even in that fervent age, for the severity of their rule. Among the many abbeys which he founded in Ireland were those of Doire Calgaigh,

* The modern Derry, or Londonderry.

Durrow, Swords, and Kells,—all houses famous in the ecclesiastical annals of Erinn. "In the forty-second year of his age, (563,) St Columba, resolving to seek a foreign country for the love of Christ, sailed from Ireland to Britain,"* as Scotland was then called. He was graciously welcomed by Conall, king of the Albanian Scots, and a relative of his own, who gave him the island of Hy or Iona. St Columba had twelve disciples with him, and laid the foundation of the monastery of Hy, which soon became the most famous in northern Europe, and, for centuries after, the recognised head of his order. From Iona he ventured to carry the light of Christianity among the heathen, and with God's blessing he planted the standard of Christ in the Orkney Isles, in the Hebrides, among the northern Picts, and away south beyond the mountains, over the Lowlands, and into Northumbria. Amidst all these labours he found time for the cultivation of letters; and his literary productions are a title, only second to his imperishable services in the cause of God, to the gratitude and veneration of mankind. He is said to have built three hundred houses devoted to God's service, and to have written as many MS. books, some of which have survived to the present day, and are even now specimens of marvellously fine penmanship.

* Adamnan.

Adamnan, his biographer and eighth successor, has left us this portrait of him :—"Angelic in appearance, eloquent in address, holy in work, with talents of the highest order, and consummate prudence, he lived a good soldier of Christ during thirty-five years in his adopted island, (Iona.) He never could spend the space of even one hour without study or prayer, or writing, or some other holy occupation ; and so incessantly was he engaged night and day in the unwearied exercise of watching and of corporal austerities, that the weight of his singular labour would seem beyond the power of human endurance; and still he was beloved by all, for a holy joy ever beaming in his face revealed the ecstasies with which the Holy Spirit filled his inmost soul." Baithen, the immediate successor of St Columba in the abbacy of Hy, was a relative of the saint, and a native of Tyrconnell. Adamnan also, from whom we have quoted so much, was a native of Tyrconnell, and was himself a saint, and one of the most remarkable men of his time. Sprung from the stock of the renowned Conall-Gulben, he seems to have devoted himself from his earliest years to the service of God, in the order of his more renowned kinsman St Columbkille. In due time he was elected to the abbacy of Hy, being the ninth in order from the holy founder. His talents and accomplishments, as well as his extraordinary sanctity, made themselves known under the rude garb of the monk, and kings and legislators often invoked his assistance in matters of difficulty. He seems to have lived much in Ireland. He was the intimate friend of the famous Alfrid of North Britain. At a legislative assembly at Tara, in the year 697, he procured the passing of the law of the innocents, viz., a law protecting women and children from the barbarities of war,—a law afterwards known as the Canon of Adamnan, a memorial which a conqueror of the world might envy. The venerable Bede bears testimony, and a more competent witness there could not be, that he was "a good man, and wise, and a peer in the knowledge of the Scriptures."[*]

Aodh Ainmire, the monarch who held the Convention of the states of Erinn at Drumceat, was of the race of Conall. The love between the patriarch brothers, Eoghan and Conall, was literally strong as death, but it did not descend through their posterity in unruffled stream. The history of their children is from the first checkered by alternations of close alliance and friendship one day, and fierce battle the next. Yet, though their records present

---

[*] "Vir bonus et sapiens, et scientia Scripturarum nobilissimè instructus." H. E., lib. 5, c. 15.

specimens of the bad sufficiently frequent and re-
volting, they are redeemed by as much of the good
and the noble as the reader of history will find in
the course of any section of the children of men.
Grianan of Aileach, on the hill of the same name overlooking the Swilly, was long the chief residence of
the princes of the northern branch of the stock of
Niall, who for many centuries shared the monarchy
of Erinn alternately with the collateral branch, the
southern Hy-Niall.

The tourist will meet many a Danish fort in Tyrconnell. We find Niall Caille, son of Hugh (Aeodh)
Oirduigh (the Legislator,) taking a lead (811) in the
reaction against the Danes, on whom he inflicted
a severe defeat at Derry ; and fifty years later,
(864,) Hugh Finliath, of the same race, defeated
them at Lough Foyle, and elsewhere. The bards of
his time celebrate in immortal verse this brave and
chivalrous Hugh ; and they sing with a still warmer
inspiration the exploits of his gallant son, Niall
Glundubh, (of the Black-knee,) who, after many a
valorous deed, fell, while yet in the prime of life, in
an engagement with the Danes. Niall left a son
worthy of himself, by name Muirkertoch, "a man
of heroic and generous spirit, willing to sacrifice
every personal feeling for his country." *   This

* Haverty's Hist. of Ireland, p. 130.

northern chieftain was the most formidable enemy
the Danes had yet met in Ireland.   He attacked
them in their strongholds in the Hebrides ; and, to
unite all the princes of Irish blood in the country
in one common cause against the pagan Norsemen,
he made that famous " Circuit of Ireland," celebrated
by bard and annalist.   Beginning with Ath Cliath,
(Dublin,) the Danish metropolis, the bold Muirkertoch swept all before him, carrying Sitric, brother
of the king of the Danes, from Ath Cliath, Lorcan,
king of Leinster, Callaghan, king of Munster, and
Conor, king of Connaught, back with him to
Aileach ; and, after celebrating there his victory
for five months, handed these royal hostages over
to Donough, then monarch of Ireland, (939.)
Finally, " the Hector of the west of Europe," as
Muirkertoch was styled by the annalists, fell fighting against his inveterate foes, the Danes, at Ardee,
941.   Cathbar, (Caffar,) the head of the Cinel-
Conall, took the name of O'Donnell from his grandfather, Donnell, who flourished in 950, and this was
the first O'Donnell.   Donnell, son and successor of
Muirkertoch, adopted the surname O'Neil from
his grandfather, Niall Glundubh, and this was the
first instance of a hereditary surname in Ireland.
Soon after, pursuant to an ordinance of Brian
Boroimhe, permanent surnames were adopted by

the various families of the population, the head of
each family taking for surname the name of his
father, or some other notable amongst his ancestors.
In the year 1010, the celebrated Brian, after a long
and difficult struggle, reduced the northern Hy-Niall
to an acquiescence in his sovereignty ; and the next
year took the lord of Cinel-Conall, the last to give in,
prisoner, and carried him to his palace at Kincora.
But the proud spirit of the northern princes did not
long submit to Dalcassian ascendancy.   O'Loughlin,
the king of Aileach, and the representative of the
northern Hy-Niall, asserted his claim to the monarchy of Erinn at the head of an army, with which
he marched to, and attacked Brian's palace at Kincora.   Murtough O'Brien, who was a man of great
capacity, and whose resources were ample, put forth
all his strength to maintain the supremacy so hardly
won by the great Brian.   The Irish annals of the
latter part of this century and the early part of the
next are full of the incidents of the fierce struggle.
O'Loughlin succeeded in destroying the palace at
Kincora.   In 1101, O'Brien set out in person at the
head of a great army, composed of drafts from
all the other provinces, and marched to the north,
crossed into Tyrconnell at Ballyshannon, thence to
Inishowen, destroying as he went, and, in return for
the attack of O'Loughlin on Kincora, took a Dal-

cassian's revenge on the Grianan of Aileach, which he razed to the ground, and commanded that a stone from it should be put into each sack that had been used for carrying provisions for the army, and brought to build a battlement on his castle at Limerick, whither he returned after having made a circuit of Ireland in six weeks, without meeting an enemy to dispute his passage. This, however, did not involve the destruction of the power of Donal O'Loughlin, whom the annalists call Monarch of Erinn, up till his death in the year 1120, or 1121. The contest between the two chiefs was never regularly fought out, though it lasted through half a century.

About the middle of the twelfth century, a hardly less formidable rival for the first place amongst the rulers of Erinn appeared in the O'Connor, a house that had grown powerful in Connaught. The war, which was of the fiercest kind, both by sea and land, was not yet over when the Anglo-Normans appeared on the scene. It is a mistake to regard the invasion of the Anglo-Normans (1169) as a war between the English on one side, and the Irish on the other. It was a war between Irish chiefs themselves in which the Anglo-Norman knights took part, as the auxiliaries or allies of one side. The numerous hereditary feuds of the princes, as well as the impulsive

character of the Irish race, created a great demand
for the sword of the stranger, and the Anglo-Norman,
being brave and unscrupulous, exacted a large payment in land, and held it. Bodies of the adven-
turers established themselves at Slane and Kells, in
Meath, whence they issued from time to time to
plunder their neighbours in the north. Suddenly
MacLoughlin, with his Kinel-Eoghan, bore down
on them, attacked the castle of Slane, and slew all
there at the time to the number of five hundred.
The other castles were quickly evacuated. Famous
amongst all the English knights was John de Courcey. To the physical strength of a giant he added
a spirit of daring and enterprise beyond most
knights of that adventurous age. He claimed
Ulster as his own, and marched with a band of men
after his own heart to make good his claim. His
first raid was into Down, where he succeeded at
first in establishing himself, (1177.) But in the ten
years that followed he suffered severe disasters from
the Kinel-Owen and the Kinel-Conall. In 1188
MacLoughlin of Aileach defeated the English with
great slaughter in Tyrone. The year after De Courcey set out on an expedition against Tyrconnell,
(1189,) but was so roughly handled by the Kinel-
Conall, under the O'Muldorey, who were before him
at Ballysadare, in the county of Sligo, that he re-

treated precipitately, and betook himself to Leinster. Some seven years later, the same O'Muldorey, now become chief of the Kinel-Eoghan and the Kinel-Conall, defeated the English at Coleraine; but dying soon after, O'Doherty became chieftain of Kinel-Conall, and was killed in a fierce encounter with De Courcey on the hill of Knoc-Noscain, near Lough Swilly, in Inishowen. And now again came on a fresh outburst of the fearful contest between the Kinel-Conall and Kinel-Eoghan, during which time the English were able to establish themselves in a castle at Caol Uisge, on the Erne, near the present village of Belleek. After a decade of fighting, Hugh O'Neil and Donnell Mor O'Donnell, the chiefs of Tyrone and Tyrconnell, settled their old differences to make common cause against the English, beat them in two or three engagements, and captured the castle at Caol Uisge, (1210.) This Donnell Mor O'Donnell made good his claim to the chieftaincy over Northern Connaught.

The English barons had long set their hearts on crushing Tyrconnell. Maurice Fitzgerald, then Lord Justice of Ireland, and one of the boldest and bravest of the Anglo-Norman knights, contrived, through the aid of O'Connor, one of his Irish auxiliaries, to cross the ford at Ballyshannon, and to hold his ground there at a time when Godfrey O'Donnell

and Rory O'Cananan were contesting the chieftainship of Tyrconnell. But the Tyrconnellians made
peace, and drove the English far beyond their borders. A few years afterwards, Maurice Fitzgerald once
more led his mailed warriors against Tyrconnell.
Godfrey O'Donnell went out to meet him. (1257.)
The armies encountered each other at Creadran-
Kille, in the north of Sligo. They fought long and
fiercely. Fitzgerald and O'Donnell met in single
combat. O'Donnell clove his antagonist to the earth,
and the powerful baron was carried off the field to
die. O'Donnell, too, received a death-wound in the
encounter. The victory remained with the Irish,
and the English fled from Lower Connaught. The
chief of the O'Neils took advantage of the dying
condition of Godfrey to assert the supremacy of
the Kinel-Owen over the Kinel-Conall. He sent
to demand hostages ; and they who came on this
dangerous errand fled for their lives the instant they
delivered the message. O'Donnell answered by
ordering a muster of his fighting men. The
strength of O'Neil marched towards the Swilly.
The dying chieftain had himself placed in the coffin
in which he was to be buried, and was thus carried
out at the head of his army. Both armies met
at Conwall, within a mile of the present Letterkenny. The Kinel-Conall triumphed, and the

B

heroic spirit of Godfrey departed amid the shouts of victory.

The years that followed were years of hard fighting between the O'Donnells and the neighbouring chieftains; and each year as it passed witnessed fresh proofs of the indomitable spirit of Clan-Conall. True, the annals of those years are checkered by many a dark crime—and where is the history that may not be reduced to a catalogue of crimes?—but by the side of their contemporaries the lords of Tyrconnell appear to advantage. Most of the chieftains of those days who did not die gloriously on the field of battle, died, to use the beautiful phraseology of the annals, "in the religious habit, after the victory of penance."

During the second half of the fourteenth century, they were able to turn the tide of war against the O'Neils, and the standard with the "In hoc signo vinces" of O'Donnell waved in triumph over many a field in Tyrone. In 1428 Niall O'Donnell, surnamed Garbh, (the Bold,) and the O'Neils, combined against the English in Ulster, and with one or two other northern chieftains, were able to levy black-rent on all the English colonists up to Meath. Two years afterwards, (1433,) the O'Neils and O'Donnells waged a terrific war against each other, but in the following year they once more united against the English. Owing to an imprudence of the young O'Neil, Niall Garbh, (the Bold,) the bravest man of his time, fell into the hands of the enemy. The English, rejoiced at getting possession of their most formidable foe, sent him to the Tower of London. He died five years afterwards (1439) in the Isle of Man, whither he had been removed to make arrangements for the payment of a ransom with which he had agreed to purchase his liberty. He left sons who were basely disinherited by his brother Naghten; but after an interval of some years they found means to put an end to their uncle, and one of them, Hugh Roe, was installed in the chieftainship. It was he who had in 1474 founded the historic monastery of Franciscans at Donegal. He greatly distinguished himself in a war against the O'Neils, whom he severely chastised in their own territory. (1493.) In 1495 we find him on a visit to the king of Scotland, where he was received with the greatest honour. The Scotch writers of the time speak of him as " the Great O'Donnell." Soon after, there was sad work in Tyrconnell, for the sons of Hugh Roe had differed, and in spite of all their father could do to the contrary, carried their disputes to the arbitrament of the sword. O'Neil, taking advantage of the weakened, (because divided,) strength of

his old enemy, invaded Tyrconnell, and gained a
temporary success in the district of Fanad.   In
1499 we find the courtly O'Donnell visiting Garret,
Earl of Kildare, the "great earl, valorous, princely,
and religious," the then Lord-deputy of Ireland;
and we may gather the consideration in which
Hugh Roe was held by the earl from the fact that
the latter gave him his son in fosterage.   Next
year we find Hugh Roe and Kildare marching together to the north to settle some difference between the O'Neils, and three years after (1504,) we
find him with the men of Tyrconnell marching
with Kildare against the Burkes of Connaught and
several other princes who were their allies.   On the
19th of August was fought the battle of Knocktow,
(Knoc Tuagh, the Hill of Axes,) "one of the most
sanguinary and decisive battles since the invasion,"
and the most important blow ever struck for the
establishment of the power of the Pale.   The earl
seems to have followed throughout this important
campaign the guidance of the veteran O'Donnell.
Not an Englishman was hurt in this battle, say the
British accounts; "and no wonder," adds a historian, "for it is probable a single Englishman
was not employed in the battle."   In 1505
Hugh Roe died.   "In his time," say the annalists,
"there was no need of defence for the houses

of Tyrconnell, except to close the doors against the wind."

Hugh Oge, or Hugh Duv, succeeded; and he, too, stood Kildare in good stead in a war against the O'Briens. This prince went in the year 1511 on a pilgrimage to Rome. O'Neil took advantage of his absence to make a raid into Tyrconnell, for which O'Donnell made him pay very dearly on his return. In the year 1513 he visited Scotland, and was treated with great honour by James IV., who, we are told, had determined on invading Ireland, but was dissuaded from the enterprise by O'Donnell. Next year he made good his claim to the sovereignty over Inishowen, Fermanagh, and other tracts formerly belonging to the O'Neils; and, two years afterwards, he extended his sway up to Sligo. He employed cannon in his successful attack on the castle of Sligo, the first use of artillery we read of in Ireland. The Earl of Surrey writes of him to his master, Henry VIII., (1520,) "I fynde him a right wise man," and not long after he writes of both O'Donnell and O'Neil, that "it would be dangerful to have them both agreed," and that "the longer they continue in war the better it should be for your grace's poor subjects here." It was a terrible war that between O'Neil and O'Donnell. O'Neil had the address to create a powerful coalition

against the growing power of Tyrconnell. There
were almost all the princes of Connaught, English
as well as Irish; there were the O'Briens and
O'Kennedys from the distant Thomond; there
were quotas from Meath and Leinster; there were
the men of Oriel and Fermanagh; and there was a
Scottish legion under Alexander MacDonnell of the
Isles, who all came to fight on the side of Tyrone.
O'Donnell called his clans, and they came — the
O'Boyles, the O'Dohertys, the MacSweenys, the
O'Gallahers, and some other branches of the Clan-
Conall—a small phalanx compared with the array
against them. O'Donnell awaited his enemy on
the east bank of the Foyle, opposite Lifford, the
usual pass between Tyrone and Tyrconnell. But
O'Neil entered by another route, and laid waste
the country as far as Ballyshannon. However,
after some marches and counter-marches, both
armies encamped over against each other at Knock-
Budhbh, or Knocavoe, near Strabane. O'Donnell
took the initiative by a night attack, which resulted
in an utter rout of O'Neil, with the loss of nine
hundred men. The victorious chief next marched
rapidly across the country to Sligo, where a body
of O'Neil's allies besieged his castle. The besiegers
broke up and fled at his approach. The result of
this brief campaign added immensely to the renown

of O'Donnell, who now turned towards Tyrone, where he was committing fearful depredations, until Kildare, coming with O'Neil, induced them to make a truce, and in 1526 invited them to an assembly of the nobles at Dublin to adjust their differences. Hugh O'Donnell was represented at this assembly by his son, Manus; but all efforts to bring about a peace were in vain; and the war between Tyrone and Tyrconnell went on fiercely as before. Manus O'Donnell built, in spite of the O'Neils, a strong frontier castle at the pass at Lifford, called Port-na-dtri-namhad, and it was here, a few years later, he wrote an Irish life of the famous St Collum-Cille. The veteran Hugh Dhu O'Donnell died in the monastery at Donegal in 1537. "He did not suffer the English to come into his country," say the Four Masters, "but he made a league of peace and friendship with the king of England when he saw that the Irish would not yield superiority to any one among themselves, but that friends and blood-relations contended against each other."

He was succeeded by his son Manus, who married the Lady Eleanor MacCarthy, the famous aunt of Gerald, the representative of the house of Kildare— a marriage that gained for the infant Gerald a safe asylum in Tyrconnell after the execution of Silken Thomas and his uncles.

It had now become the fashion among the Irish chieftains to seek to stand well with the English, and O'Donnell, though late, began to show a leaning in the same direction. Accordingly, he crossed the Channel in 1542, to pay his respects to Henry VIII., and we find a courtly writer of the day marking him out by his " coat of crimson velvet, with twenty or thirty pairs of golden aiglets, his great double cloak of crimson satin, bordered with black velvet, his bonnet with a feather set full of aiglets of gold." He had a grant of the title of Earl of Tyrconnell, but it remained in abeyance until 1603. Meanwhile there was treason in Tyrconnell. Calvagh rose in red rebellion against his own father, Manus, and O'Cane came to join him ; but they were defeated in 1548, in a battle at Srath-bo-Fiach, now Bally-bofey, on the river Finn. But the spirit of revolt endured. Other chieftains owing obedience to O'Donnell rebelled, and invoked the assistance of the English, which the latter, true to their traditional policy, eagerly accorded. Calvagh O'Donnell, not yet entirely subdued, once more took the field against his father, this time with success, owing to the assistance of a body of Scottish auxiliaries whom he got to join his standard. He took Manus prisoner, and had him confined in one of his castles.

But before long this unnatural son sorely needed

the advice of his ill-used father, for there had arisen
in Tyrone one O'Neil, surnamed Shane the Proud, a
man of impetuous, fiery temper, and of great ambition, who thought there was now a favourable opportunity for asserting the superiority claimed by
O'Neil over Tyrconnell. The experienced Manus
counselled his son to oppose his adversary rather
by stratagem than in a pitched battle. Accordingly,
O'Donnell hovered on the march of the redoubtable
Shane, till at a fit moment, while O'Neil lay encamped one night at Balleehan, near Raphoe, he
attacked the camp, which he entered without resist-
ance, and slaughtered all that came in his way,
O'Neil having narrowly escaped through the back
of his tent, and fled with but two or three attend-
ants back to his own territory. (1558.) Shane
O'Neil, however, soon recovered from the shock of
this reverse. It was a sufficient *casus belli* for him
against Tyrconnell that the English, with whom he
was then at war, had about this time sent a friendly
message to O'Donnell. With the characteristic rapidity of his movements, he descended upon Tyrconnell, and came suddenly on Calvagh, who, with
some members of his family, was then staying at
the monastery of Killydonnell, on Lough Swilly,
almost unattended, his army being away on some
duty in the wild neighbourhood of Lough Veagh.

The Tyrone chief had thus a cheap triumph, and hastened back to his own territory, carrying with him O'Donnell and his wife. Calvagh was ransomed two years after, and the Lord-deputy Sussex came at the head of an armed force into Tyrconnell, to reinstate him in his castles and strongholds.

Three years later he was succeeded by his brother Hugh, in whom Shane O'Neil found the most stern as well as the most able opponent he had yet encountered. Hugh determined to resist O'Neil's arrogant claims to superiority, and of this he gave most unmistakable proofs, by two attacks on Tyrone. The haughty Shane, fired with indignation, once more set out to take summary vengeance on the new chief of Tyrconnell. He crossed the Swilly at low water, two miles below Letterkenny. Hugh, with his small force, awaited him in position at Ardnagarry, on the northern side. The attack was fierce beyond description. For a while the cause of Tyrconnell seemed lost, but the able generalship of Hugh, and the stubborn, unfaltering resolution of the Clan Conall prevailed against immense odds, and the men of Tyrone were driven back into the returning tide. The loss of O'Neil is variously stated at from 1300 to 3000 men. Shane himself fled barely with his life up the river, which he succeeded in crossing near Scariff-Hollis, and made his way back to Tyrone. He never recovered from this blow.

In 1584, Sir John Perrott assumed the Lord-deputyship of Ireland, and the following year is memorable for a parliament assembled by him at Dublin. The Four Masters, in their list of the septs present on this occasion, set down Hugh O'Neil in the first place, then Hugh O'Donnell, chief of Tyrconnell. Other names from Tyrconnell figure in the list, viz., John Oge O'Doherty, chief of Inishowen ; Turlough O'Boyle, chief of Boylagh ; Owen O'Gallaher, O'Donnell's marshal. On this occasion the accomplished Hugh O'Neil cultivated the friendship of the O'Donnell, whose daughter he received in marriage.

Perrott first divided Ulster into counties, for each of which sheriffs, commissioners of the peace, and coroners were nominated. It was decreed that Tyrconnell should henceforth be the county of Donegal. O'Donnell, who all through his reign had been the staunch friend of the English, indignantly resisted this interference with the autonomy of Tyrconnell. He refused to admit the English sheriff into his district. The council at Dublin were in a difficulty. A war with Tyrconnell was the last thing to be wished just now. Perrott, it is said, prided himself on his fertility of expedients. Hugh O'Donnell was

now old and feeble ; but there was growing up to
him a son, another Hugh, who, though yet a mere
stripling, had already given such promise as made
him famous in the land.   The youth was then staying in Fanad with his foster-father, MacSweeny.   A
ship, well supplied with foreign wines, put into
Lough Swilly, and cast anchor opposite Rathmullen
Castle.   Communications were opened with the
people on the shore.   It was given out that she was
a Spanish trader in wines.   The crew being good
fellows, and their terms liberal, the people of the
district eagerly sought to board the Spanish ship.
The young O'Donnell and a few of his more intimate companions came on board at the urgent invitation of the hospitable master.   They were enter-
tained in royal style ; but while partaking of the
good things set before them in the cabin, the hatches
were closed down, the young men disarmed, the
cable slipped, and the sails spread to the wind.   The
ship stood out to sea, and in due time arrived at
Dublin.   Sir John Perrott, highly delighted with
the success of his scheme, consigned his prize to the
dungeons of Dublin Castle.   After more than three
years in that close prison, he contrived (1590) to
get swung down from one of the windows of the
castle, late on a winter's evening, and get through
the gates of the city unobserved.   Crossing the Three-

Rock Mountain, after the hardship of a night's wandering in the mountains beyond, which had nearly cost him his life, he found shelter with Felim O'Toole of Wicklow. The Government soldiers, who were in close pursuit, easily traced the young O'Donnell to his asylum. O'Toole was not able to protect him, and the young prince was brought back to his old prison. But his brother-in-law, the wary Hugh O'Neil, had an eye on him. Perrott had been succeeded in the lord-deputyship by Sir William Fitzwilliam, "a man of cruel and sordid disposition." There is reason to believe that Fitzwilliam's vigilance relaxed under O'Neil's gold. Two years after his first attempt at escape, the young O'Donnell, with two young O'Neils, (luckless princes!) also long confined in that prison, effected an egress through a sewer of the castle, and, joined in the street by a guide stationed there by Hugh O'Neil, hurried through the city. One of the young O'Neils strayed from the party in the streets. The other, with O'Donnell and the guide, struck out in the direction of the Three-Rock Mountain, which they crossed, and pursued their way over the Wicklow mountains towards the castle of Fiagh Hugh O'Byrne, in Glenmalure. It was Christmas night. A severe frost had set in, and a blinding snow-storm overtook them on their difficult way over that wild region, all which proved too much for the youths, scantily clad, and with strength already wasted by a long and hard imprisonment. They were obliged at length to succumb. The servant hastened alone to Glenmalure with the sad news. O'Byrne made haste to send succour. A troop of his hardy men sped fleetly in their errand to the spot where the servant had left the youths. "The bodies of the young princes were covered with white-bordered shrouds of hailstones freezing around them, and their light clothes adhered to their skin, so that, covered as they were with the snow, it did not appear to the men who had arrived that they were human beings at all, for they found no life in their members, but just as if they were dead."* On being lifted from the ground, Art O'Neill fell back and expired. Hugh Roe slowly revived, and was carried insensible to Glenmalure.

Impatient to get to the North, as soon as he was able to sit on horseback, he set out, and, eluding the English, who were on the watch for him along every route northward through the Pale, he reached Dungannon, whence, after a short stay with O'Neil, he proceeded to his father's castle at Ballyshannon. He had travelled fast, but his fame had travelled faster. The clans of Tyrconnell assembled in great numbers

* Annals of the Four Masters.

on the banks of the Saimer* to greet this "son of prophecy."

It was not long before the young Hugh Roe gave a specimen of the stuff that was in him. Two English officers had seized the monastery of Donegal, whence they overawed the country round. Though still suffering from the effects of that dreadful night in the Wicklow mountains, Hugh Roe was up betimes the next morning after his arrival, and, mustering a force from the clansmen that had come to welcome him home, marched at their head to Donegal. The enemy fled at his approach, and he returned to Ballyshannon, having re-established the friars in their monastery. Now at length, he was fain to submit his frost-bitten feet to the treatment of the physicians, who found it necessary to amputate both his great toes. Early in April old Sir Hugh resigned, whereupon the young Hugh Roe was elected to the chieftaincy amid universal acclamations. The young prince delayed not a moment to proclaim eternal hostility to the English. The first object of his attack was Sir Tirlough O'Neil, a chieftain who maintained the English interest in Tyrone, whom he speedily subdued, (1593,) and forced to resign all claim to the title of chief of the O'Neil, and to dismiss his

* The old name for the river Erne.

English guard, so that now once more the O'Neil and O'Donnell were supreme in Ulster. Then he took the side of MacGuire of Fermanagh, against the English, and the arm of Tyrconnell enabled that chief to achieve a glorious triumph over the united forces of the Pale and some Irish allies.

He opened the next campaign (1594) with the invasion of Connaught, where the English authority had long been paramount, and whence Governor Bingham, a man whose barbarities were so flagrant as to procure his recall by Elizabeth, had lately issued to plunder the coasts of Tyrconnell. At the head of his little army, probably not numbering more than one English regiment of the present day, but all fired with the spirit of their young captain, and excited by the fresh air and exercise, descended through the passes of Northern Connaught, and in two months destroyed every English settlement all the way to Annally.* Next year (1595) we again find him exercising royal powers in Connaught, adjudicating on the disputed titles of chieftains, restoring to their property the people that had been dispossessed by Bingham, destroying castles where the English might again get a footing. Towards the close of this year, a Connaught chieftain, O'Connor of Sligo, returned after a long stay in England, and

---

* Co. Longford.

joined with zealous loyalty in all the measures of
Sir Conyers Clifford, the successor of Bingham.
Clifford's character was exactly the opposite of
Bingham's. Brave, generous, and humane, he soon
grew into popularity. The English interest rose
once more. O'Donnell was indignant. In cold
December he crossed the river Sligo, and drove off
every head of cattle belonging to those who had
joined O'Connor; and in the following month he
returned with a larger force, and swept all Connaught, as far as the walls of Galway, and then returned northward, to reverse all that had been done
by Clifford and O'Connor.

Meanwhile, the English were not idle. Late in
July, Sir Conyers Clifford, having mustered all the
royalist forces of Connaught at Boyle, marched to
Sligo, thence to the Erne, which he crossed at a ford
near Belleek, and laid siege to the castle of Ballyshannon. He had cannon sent round to him by sea
from Galway. The castle, defended by a garrison of
only eighty soldiers, bravely repulsed every assault
till O'Donnell arrived, when the game was reversed,
and the besiegers were themselves besieged. At
the early dawn of the 15th of August, the English
silently crossed a ford of the Erne, a little above the
cataract of Asharoe, and retreated at full speed to
Sligo, leaving three pieces of ordnance and all the

military stores to Hugh Roe, (1597,) who, from this time, seems to have made Ballymote his head-quarters, whence he was able to stretch his arm over Connaught and Tyrconnell, as need might be. His residence at Ballymote was a castle which had been in the hands of the royalists, and therefore fell to O'Donnell by the right of war; but it is worth noting, as an illustration of the character of this Bayard of Tyrconnell, that he paid MacDonagh, the original owner of the place, the full value of the property—viz., £400 sterling and 300 cows.

In 1598, O'Neil needed the arm of Tyrconnell. Hugh Roe came gladly at his call, and what with the prestige of his name, and the soul-stirring effu-sions of his poet Fearfesa O'Clery, and the resolution of his men, he contributed in great measure to Hugh O'Neil's important victory over the English at Beal-an-atha-buy, or the mouth of the Yellow Ford, two miles from Armagh. "It was a glori-ous victory for the rebels," says the contemporary English historian Camden, "and of special advan-tage : for hereby they got arms and provisions, and Tyrone's name was cried up all over Ireland as the author of their liberty." At the close of this year we find O'Donnell once more scouring the territory of Clanrickarde, the zealous ally of the English, and in the spring following, (1599,) he visited the distant Thomond, also in close alliance with the English.

Essex landed this year in Ireland with 20,000 foot and 2,000 horse—an immense army compared with that of the Ulster confederates. O'Connor of Sligo declared for him, at which O'Donnell was very wroth. He hastened to call the Connaught chieftain to account. O'Connor fled before him from post to post, till he was at last cooped up in his castle at Coloney. Essex ordered Clifford to hasten to his relief. Accordingly, Clifford set out with a well-appointed force from Athlone. Hugh Roe hearing of his approach, drew off as many men as could be spared from the siege, and went to meet him. They encountered each other in the gap of Ballaghboy, in the Curliew mountains. The odds against O'Donnell were heavy in the important matter of numbers and equipments, but he had the selection of the ground. The English advanced at a measured and steady pace. The men of Tyrconnell charged them with such impetuosity, that they recoiled at the first shock. The battle was soon over. O'Donnell pressed hotly and fiercely; the English column broke and fled. Amongst the slain the body of Sir Conyers Clifford was recognised, and treated with great honour by the chivalrous Hugh. After this victory O'Connor surrendered, and the generous

O'Donnell's revenge was to reinstate him in his territory, and even to give him cattle to stock his lands.

On the 16th of May in this year, an English fleet of sixty-seven sail, carrying 4000 foot and 200 horse —a force stronger than the entire army of Ulster— under the command of Sir Henry Dowcra, entered Lough Foyle. Simultaneously with this, Mountjoy, the lord-deputy, lately arrived from England, made a feint against Ulster by the Blackwater, thus drawing off the attention of O'Neil and O'Donnell from Dowcra, until the latter had time to fortify himself at Derry. Part of Dowcra's plan was to send a detachment of 1000 foot and 50 horse by sea to Ballyshannon, but this project he had to abandon at the time, as he had quite enough to do to keep his post behind his strong fortifications at Derry. As he could not tempt the English to venture beyond their lines, Hugh Roe left Nial Garv O'Donnell to watch them, while he himself set out against Clanrickarde and Thomond. This time he swept almost the whole of Clare, and again appeared before Derry in an incredibly short space of time. At the end of July, this almost ubiquitous general encountered Dowcra in a sortie, in which the English general was beaten, and pursued up to the very walls of the fortress. Dowcra after this remained within his lines ; and O'Donnell being needed elsewhere, he left Nial Garv with a force of observation before Derry, and set out once more against the obnoxious Dalcassian, who styled himself Earl of Thomond. Swiftly and silently he bore down on that devoted territory, and swept all Thomond from Corcomroe to Loop-Head.

But a dark shadow now fell across his path. Nial Garv joined the enemy. This Nial, who was brother-in-law to Hugh Roe, and his kinsman, inherited the traditions and claims to the chieftaincy of Calvagh O'Donnell, whose grandson he was. His wife, Nuala, the heroic sister of Hugh Roe, left him on his traitorous defection to the English. He was a very brave man, and rendered good service to the English, as Dowcra himself owned.

Immediately on his defection he marched with 1000 men to Lifford, and took possession of the then O'Donnell's castle for the English. The sad intelligence reached Hugh Roe at Ballymote. He flew to Lifford. The sturdy Nial with his 1000 men held the castle. Hugh Roe assailed it, but in vain. It was now winter, and his soldiers were worn by the fatigues of their marvellously active campaign, and so, all-impatient as he was, he had to put off the reckoning with his false cousin and officer to another day.

With the summer of 1601 came new trials to
O'Donnell. The young Earl of Clanrickarde was
once more in arms at the head of a powerful army.
Hugh Roe marched against him. Nial Garv took
advantage of his absence to march to Donegal with
a body of 500 English from Dowcra, and seize
the monastery, which he fortified. O'Donnell having disposed of Clanrickarde, hastened to Donegal,
and laid siege to the monastery. Nial held out
with his usual stubborn courage. He was supported
by an English ship in the harbour. On the night of
the 19th September a fire broke out in the building.
It was a fit moment for Hugh to make an assault,
which he did, the garrison contesting every point.
The struggle lasted all through the night. In the
early morning Nial, with the survivors of the garrison,
retreated under cover of the ship in the harbour
along the strand to the neighbouring abbey at Magherabeg. Hugh Roe followed speedily, but Nial
resisted his renewed attacks with his usual uncon-
querable resolution, and still held the place, when
couriers arrived in Hugh Roe's camp with a message
to the effect that an expedition sent by the king of
Spain to aid the Irish against Elizabeth had arrived
at Kinsale, and waited to be joined there by the
Irish princes, especially O'Neil and O'Donnell.
Hugh Roe, leaving Nial in possession of the walls

of Magherabeg, prepared to join the Spaniards. He was the first of the northern chieftains on the way to Kinsale. At the head of about 2500 men, drawn from Tyrconnell and Northern Connaught, he set out about the end of October. When he reached Ikerrin, in the county of Tipperary, he found that Sir George Carew, with a much superior force, lay across his path in the plain of Cashel, while St Lawrence was in rapid pursuit in his rear with the army of the Pale. A high difficult mountain rose up on his right, so that he was hemmed in on every side. But O'Donnell was not to be stayed. He resolved to cross Slieve Phelim, impassable though it appeared, and a heavy frost setting in during the night greatly facilitated his progress. Carew having received information of the detour, set out to intercept him, but by the time he reached Kilmallock Hugh Roe had got so far as Croom, having marched in one day thirty-two Irish miles over the roughest ground imaginable, " the greatest march," writes Carew, " with carriage that hath been heard of."* Sir George, thinking it folly to try to cope with "so swift-footed a general," as he expressed it, returned direct to the camp of Mountjoy, who lay before Kinsale. On the 21st of December, O'Neil, O'Donnell, and one or two Munster chieftains, encamped on the heights of Bel-

* Pacata Hibernia.

goley, north of Kinsale. The besieging army was now itself besieged, and the veteran O'Neil saw that, cut off as it was from supplies from every quarter, every hour that passed made its defeat surer. But the captain of the Spaniards had sent messages pressing an attack on the English camp while he should make a sortie from the town. O'Donnell, roused by some cutting observations of the Spaniard, more than by the natural impetuosity of his character, recommended an immediate attack. A council of war was called, and Hugh Roe carried the majority against the better judgment of O'Neil. During the night of the 23d, the Irish army was set in motion. Just before daybreak the first division, broken by the difficult nature of the ground and the darkness, suddenly found themselves confronted by the enemy standing under arms in excellent order. Then ensued not a battle, but a carnage. When O'Donnell, who was following far in the rear, came up, the panic had become general. He called on the men to stand and fight the enemy, "until his voice and speech," as the annalists express it, "were strained by the vehemence and loudness of the language in which he addressed all in general, requesting his nobles to stand by him and fight their enemies." * But all in vain. The disorder was irretrievable.

* Annals of the Four Masters, anno 1601.

O'Neil and O'Donnell retreated to Inishannon, near Bandon. The annalists counted the loss in killed and wounded as a trifle compared with the loss of prestige. This reverse seems to have depressed the susceptible spirit of Hugh Roe to a degree which it is hard to realise. "He was seized," say the annalists, "with great fury, rage, and anxiety of mind; so that he did not sleep or rest soundly for the space of three nights."* The Spanish expedition had been a mismanaged affair altogether. The force sent was not strong enough; it landed at the spot where the English power was strongest, and the Irish weakest; the leader, though brave, held an insulting tone to the Irish, whom he did not take the trouble to understand. Hugh Roe resolved to proceed to Spain in person to press King Philip III. to follow up this expedition by another under better auspices, and O'Neil reluctantly agreed to the proposal. Accordingly, he delegated the chieftainship of the Cinel-Conal to his brother Rory in his absence, and sailed from Castlehaven, followed by "the loud clapping of hands, pitiful and mournful to hear, the intense tearful moaning, and the loud wailing lamentation"† of his men, and was wafted by a favourable wind to Corunna, where he was received with extraordinary

* Annals of the Four Masters, anno 1601.   † Annals, 1602.

respect, as also all along the road to Zamora, whither he hastened to catch the king, then on a tour in that part of the kingdom.

King Philip received the O'Donnell with great honour, and generously promised to have an expedition, according to his programme, fitted out immediately. Hugh Roe returned to Corunna to rest there until all things should be in readiness. The winter wore away, and the spring, and as yet no appearance of the fleet which was to sail to Ireland. Summer came and passed, and the solitary figure of the Irish chieftain might still be seen on the high beach at Corunna, looking out over the heaving element, that divided him from the country he loved so well. Not even the breeze fresh from the Atlantic could cool his blood, boiling with a fever that was now rapidly consuming him. His impatient spirit could endure the delay no longer. He started once more for the court, but died on the way, in the king's house at Simancas, and was buried with great solemnity in the Cathedral of Valladolid, on the 10th of September 1602, in the 29th year of his age.

"Thus closed the career of one of the brightest and purest characters of any history. His youth, his early captivity, his princely generosity, his daring courage, his sincere piety, won the hearts of all who came in contact with him. He was the sword, as O'Neil was the brain, of the Ulster Confederacy; the Ulysses and Achilles of the war, they fought side by side, without jealousy or envy, for almost as long a period as their prototypes had spent in besieging Troy."* The discomfiture of the northern chieftains at Kinsale gave Mountjoy an advantage which he did not fail to make the most of. He established a network of strongly garrisoned fortresses all over Ulster, and employed a large force during the summer in laying waste the country. A famine was the consequence, the details of which make one's blood run cold. On the 14th of December he received the submission of Rory, who soon afterwards accompanied him to London, where he was received with great distinction by James I. By the settlement now agreed upon, he was to remain in possession of his lordship, with the title of Earl of Tyrconnell, while the district should be subjected henceforth to the administration of the English law. O'Neil submitted on the same terms, and both returned to Ireland. They soon felt that cupidity, jealousy, religious intolerance, national antipathy, and other kindred passions, warred against them, the treaty of peace notwithstanding. They continued for a few years to pick their steps with the utmost caution. Early in

* M'Gee's History of Ireland, p. 450.

September (1607,) a packet was delivered to O'Neil while on a visit with the Lord-deputy at Slane. He took leave abruptly of his host, and proceeded in haste to the shore of Lough Swilly, where the O'Donnell awaited him. The two earls, with their families, took ship at Rathmullen, and bade adieu for ever to their inheritance. Of the party of O'Donnell were Caffar his brother, Nuala his sister, the wife of Nial Garv, whom she had left when he joined the English, his son Hugh O'Donnell, and Owen Roe MacWard, the chief bard of Tyrconnell. Rory O'Donnell died at Rome in the July following, and, two months later, his brother Caffar was laid in the same grave with him on St Peter's Hill.

During the late crisis the English had fast friends among the O'Dohertys of Inishowen. Shortly after the flight of the earls, the young Sir Cahir, who had earned his knighthood while yet a mere lad, fighting by the side of Dowcra, was struck in the face by Sir George Paulet, the governor of Derry, during a conversation touching the flight of the earls. The O'Doherty, maddened by the indignity, seized Culmore fort on the night of the 3d of May, hastened to Derry, surprised and overpowered the garrison, slew Paulet with his own hand, and sacked the town. Of course, after the sad depletion of Tyrconnell from the late wars, he could oppose but a very slight force indeed to the trained bands of the English. Still he held out bravely for the space of three months, when he fell by a chance shot in a conflict with Marshal Wingfield and Sir Oliver Lambert, the governor of Connaught. His head was sent to Dublin.

This outburst, resulting in the early death of O'Doherty—he was only in his twenty-first year— was convenient for James I. Nial Garv and his sons, with Cormac, the brother of Hugh O'Neil, and O'Cane, were safely lodged in the dungeons of London Tower, where they rotted out the remainder of their days. Then came that favourite project of James, and the long-desired of the "undertakers," known in Irish history as the Plantation of Ulster. And on that day Tyrconnell dropped out of history.

EXCURSIONS

IN

THE DONEGAL HIGHLANDS.

BELLEEK TO BALLYSHANNON.

AFTER a sail from Enniskillen down Loch Erne, that beautiful Irish Windermere, the tourist lands at Belleek, a small village prettily situated at the western end of the lake. From this point the river Erne, formerly called the Saimer, pursues a broad and rapid course westward to the sea. A ford here was in past times one of the chief entrances into Tyrconnell, and one of the oftenest contested points, perhaps, in the history of the Irish wars. The tourist will notice on the hill above the village, a fort, now disused, and on the river below, a china manufactory. "From Belleek, the angler will be enabled to fish Loch Erne, which contains some of the finest trout in the world, running from 2 to 20 lbs. weight. These trout, up to 6 and 7 lbs. weight, take the fly well. The lough abounds also in pike, perch, and bream, of which cartloads may be taken in some spots. Flies may be had in Ballyshannon."* The declination of the bed of the river is so considerable† that the stream is broken in its course into a series of rapids, which the pedestrian would do well to explore.

* Angler's Register.
† 149 feet of incline in the four miles between Belleek and the sea.

D

The car road to Ballyshannon (4½ miles) runs nearly parallel with the river, which, however, is not always visible from it.   At a short distance from Belleek, close to the river, is Cliffe, the residence of T. Connolly, Esq., M.P., the proprietor of extensive estates in this neighbourhood, and in other parts of Donegal, and on the bank directly opposite, the antiquary will find the remains of an old church and graveyard. About two miles farther on are the remains of a castle in a field on the right, and on the left is an old "dun," called Raheen Fort.   Passing the grounds of Camlan Castle, (T. Tredenick, Esq.,) and one or two other minor residences to the right, the road gains an elevated point, whence there is a fine view of Ballyshannon.   The river rushes on in almost majestic stream, spanned by a bridge of sixteen arches, every one of which you have the satisfaction of seeing, and the town, rising abruptly from the water's edge, ascends a steep hill, surmounted by two churches, whose "silent fingers point to heaven." You now drop suddenly into the Purt, as the part of the town on the south side of the river is called, and crossing the bridge you are in the heart of

BALLYSHANNON.

There are three hotels—the Commercial, the Erne,

and Cockburn's. The tourist will see nothing to admire in the architecture of the place. There is a large-sized Protestant church, with nothing in its look to recommend it save its fine situation on the historic, or rather prehistoric, Mullaghnashee. Not less suggestive of the past is the site of the Catholic church, which holds an elevated position in the old Castle Park, a very spacious building, and abundantly rich in its internal appointments and decorations. Ballyshannon is remarkable for its excellent salmon-fishing, and is in consequence a favourite resort for the lovers of the peaceful sports of Isaak Walton. Leave to fish must be had of Dr Sheil, the lessee of the fishery, who is liberal to anglers, but they "are so numerous that it is not always possible for the proprietor to grant permission." * The trade of the town has very much declined within the past thirty years; the population is 3197, but a large proportion of the inhabitants are poor. It was incorporated by a charter of James I. (1613.) It returned two members to the Irish Parliament, from the time of its incorporation till the Union, when it was disfranchised, and the £15,000 compensation was pocketed by the Earl of Belmont.

Within three minutes' walk of any of the hotels

* Murray.

is the celebrated Fall of Ballyshannon, where the whole body of the Erne is projected over a cliff of from fourteen to sixteen feet high. This cataract exhibits a noble crest line of some 150 yards, over which the water is pretty equally distributed, and falls in a creamy sheet that contrasts finely with the black basin below. The roar is something deafening. But the Fall is hardly less interesting as a cascade than as a salmon-leap. If the tourist's visit should hit on a time when the troops of salmon in full career, rising fourteen feet at least in a spring, go bounding up that raging floodgate, he will be slow to come away from the spectacle.

This waterfall is the famous Asharoe, of which mention is so often made in Irish annals. It owes its name to an incident which heads one of the most interesting chapters in the romance of Irish history. Some three hundred years or more before the Christian era, three cousins, the sons of three brothers, claimed each for himself the kingship of Erinn. The dispute, however, was adjusted by the *Filès*, or Druids, who engaged the three claimants in a solemn compact by which each should be allowed to reign in turn for a period of seven years. Their names were Dithorba, Aedh Ruadh, and Cimbaeth,* and they lived on amicably until each had enjoyed

* Pronounced Deorba, Ec Rua, and Kimbahe.

his turn of the sovereignty three times, when Aedh Ruadh was drowned in this cataract, henceforth named *Eas-Aedh-Ruadh*, now contracted into Asharoe, that is, the cataract of Hugh Roe.* His body was recovered, and buried in the mound of Mullaghnashee, where the Protestant church now stands. Aedh left but one child, a daughter, by name Macha Mongruadh, or Macha the Red-haired. She claimed her father's right to the seven years' reign when his turn came round, but the co-sovereigns refused to allow this privilege to a woman. Whereupon, the strong-minded Macha raised an army, and after a fierce contest made good her claim by force of arms. Dithorba having been slain in the contest, and his five sons banished into the wilds of Connaught, the victorious Macha completed her triumph by marrying the remaining co-sovereign, Cimbaeth. As, however, danger was still possible from the sons of Dithorba, this energetic lady of the golden hair set out in quest of these luckless youths, and did not give over the pursuit until she had captured them among the rocks of the distant Burren. It was suggested to her to put them to death, but she was pleased to grant them their lives on the condition of their

---

* Eas, a cataract; Aedh, pronounced *ee* in Irish, and in the English *Hugh;* Ruadh, pronounced *Rua*, or *Roe*.

becoming her slaves, and she gave them for a task to build her a court, or rath, which should be thereafter the chief residence of the princes of Ulster. The queen took a golden brooch, or bodkin, with which she used to fasten her cloak round her neck, and traced out with it the foundations of the court at a place about two miles west of Armagh; and thus was begun the palace of Eomuin, so called "from *Eo*, a breastpin or brooch, and *Muin*, the neck,"* Latinised into Emania—the resort of the celebrated Red-branch Knights, and the palace of the kings of Ulster for more than eight hundred years.

From the Fall the tourist may have an easy walk to the Abbey, keeping the road along the bank for a short distance, from which he will have good views of the estuary of the Erne —a charming landscape on a bright evening. The Abbey is the name given to what remains of the monastery of Asharoe, a house of the Cistercian order of monks, founded in 1178 by Roderick O'Canannan, prince of Tyrconnell. The ruins of this sometime illustrious monastery are so scanty as hardly to preserve any one of its lineaments. Mr Allingham gives a true portrait of the Abbey of Asharoe as it is at the present day:—

* Professor O'Curry's MS. Materials of Irish History.

" A little rocky rivulet runs murmuring to the tide,
   Singing a song of ancient days in sorrow not in pride,
   The bore-tree and the lightsome ash across the portal grow,
   And heaven itself is now the roof of the Abbey Asharoe." *

The ground within the Abbey precincts has long been used as a burial-place, which, together with the sparse remains still left, is protected by a strong wall built a few years back by Dr M'Gettigan, the present Bishop of Raphoe.

The ford Athseanni, (the ancient name of Bally-shannon,) was from the oldest times regarded as the key to Tyrconnell, and here stood a famous castle of the O'Donnells. In the wars with the English, Ballyshannon was the chief point of attack. In the year 1597 Sir Conyers Clifford, at the head of twenty-two regiments of foot and ten of horse appeared suddenly on the south bank of the ford, which he crossed, and laid siege to the castle, establishing his headquarters at the monastery of Asharoe. The little garrison, consisting only of eighty men, defied all his efforts, until after a considerable interval the warriors of Tyrconnell came to their relief, when the tide of war was rolled back, and Clifford was obliged to keep within his quarters

* " Abbey Asharoe :" *Modern Poems.* Mr Allingham is a native of Ballyshannon. If our tourist be not already acquainted with "Laurence Bloomfield in Ireland," and other occasional poems by the same author, he is a loser, for there are few that have sung in so sweet or so pure a strain as William Allingham.

at the monastery. Although he was greatly aided by a train of artillery that had come to him by sea from Galway, O'Donnell's men pressed him so hotly that he soon resolved to retreat from Tyrconnell. One morning at early dawn, leaving his military stores behind him, he contrived to cross the ford a little above the Fall, but not without a large loss in men, who were carried in great numbers down the cataract. In the settlement between Rory O'Donnell and James I., in 1603, Ballyshannon and one thousand acres of the surrounding territory were reserved to the king, from which time the old castle often changed masters, till, after its capture by the Earl of Clanrickarde in 1652, it ceased any longer to be the habitation of human beings. Of this famous castle not a vestige now remains, save a piece of the old walls incorporated with some back building attached to the premises of Mr Stephens, a merchant in the town.

Distances.—Ballyshannon to Bundoran, 4 miles; to Kinlough, $6\frac{1}{2}$ miles; to Garrison, 9 miles; to Ballintra, $6\frac{1}{2}$ miles; to Donegal, $13\frac{1}{2}$ miles; to Pettigo, 17 miles.

I. Excursion to Bundoran, Kinlough, Lough Melvin, and Garrison.

Leaving Ballyshannon for Bundoran you cross

the Erne, and emerging " nothing loath " from the narrow dilapidated street of the Purt, you pursue your way over a road that has nothing in its immediate neighbourhood to interest you, but from which, as you proceed, you begin to gain fine views of sea and mountain in the distance. To the right, down amidst a waste of sandhills, are the remains of the church of Innismacsaint, from which the parish takes its name, the site of which is supposed to have been an island before the drifting of the sand. At the end of the fourth mile you arrive at

BUNDORAN, " the great north-west bathing-place, to which the rank and fashion of Ireland have been of late resorting." * The principal hotels are Hamilton's and Gallagher's. Bundoran has a commanding position on a bold coast, an extensive strand, breezes fresh from the Atlantic, good scenery to drive to, and fine views to look at in the distance, to recommend it. The place is, however, bare, and the hills too far off for the enjoyment of bathers. The view across the Donegal Bay, with its promontories of Doorin Point, and St John's Point and intervening inlets, backed up by a noble range of mountains terminating in the steep cliffs of Slieve League, is fine. A marine cave called the Fairy Bridge is

* Murray.

worth a visit. It is a narrow causeway over a natural arch twenty-four feet in span, under which the waves rush in angry tumult. From Bundoran the road is enlivened by an occasional pretty cottage as far as the Drowes river, (2 miles,) the county boundary at this part of Donegal. On the coast here is the ruined Drowes Castle, or more properly Duncarberry Castle, a stronghold built by Isabel MacClancy in the reign of Elizabeth. Beyond the Drowes, our tourist turning to the left leaves the Sligo road, to pursue that which leads up to

KINLOUGH, a small town occupying a charming situation at the west end of Lough Melvin. In the immediate neighbourhood is Kinlough House, the residence of J. Johnston, Esq., and a short way off, on the southern bank of the Lough, is Mount Prospect. To the south-west, rising abruptly from the sea, is Benbulben, the foster-home of Conall, the famous patriarch of the clans of Tyrconnell; and joined to it is Truskmore, which, stretching far inland, forms that striking mountain range that skirts the southern bank of Lough Melvin. Lough Melvin is a middle-sized lake, stretching from Kinlough seven and a half miles in an eastern direction, with a slight deflection to the south. "It contains a

spring impregnated with sulphuretted hydrogen."[*]
"There is good salmon until the middle of May,
after which grilse comes in; also splendid trout-
fishing, especially of the sort named gillaroo."[†]
Leave to fish must be had from Mr Johnston of
Kinlough House. There is a sprinkling of islands
of small size. One close to the southern shore contains the remains of the castle of Rossclogher, which
gives its name to the barony, and another on the
eastern shore contains "the ruins of the ancient
chapel of Rossinver, supposed to have been that of
the nunnery of Doiremel, founded by St Tigernach
for his mother, St Mella."[‡] The tourist may proceed by a road on the northern side of the lake, or,
if he prefer it, by that on the south, which is the
more striking but the longer road, to Garrison, a
small village with no attractions save as a resting-
place for the angler, and proceed from Garrison, by
Belleek, or by the direct road (9 miles) which
traverses a bare high ground to Ballyshannon.

II. Excursion to Kilbarron Castle.

The tourist may enjoy some good coast scenery
and at the same time gratify a very meritorious

[*] Murray.   [†] Ibid.   [‡] Lewis.

antiquarian curiosity by a visit to Kilbarron Castle, "an ancient fortress of the O'Clerys, renowned in their day for their skill in science, poetry, and history."* This castle stood on a cliff overhanging the sea, about four miles north-west of Ballyshannon, commanding a magnificent view to the north of Donegal Bay, its inlets, and its mountain barriers against the ocean, and to the south and west hardly less magnificent views of the mountain ranges of northern Connaught. The end of the lords of Kilbarron Castle, "long distinguished for hospitality, wealth, and erudition," is given by the late lamented Mr O'Donovan in the Introduction to his edition of the Four Masters, the leader of which "illustrious quartett"† was Brother Michael O'Clery of Kilbarron. Peregrine, or Cugory O'Clery, the head of the sept, was also one of the associates. In the records of the Inquisition at Lifford, in May 1632, it is stated of this O'Clery, "that being a mere Irishman, and not of English or British descent or surname, his lands were forfeited to the king." The lord of Kilbarron found a humble shelter in the county of Mayo. An extract from his will (1664) is worth repetition : "I bequeath the property most dear to me that ever I possessed in this world, namely, my books, to my two sons, Dermott and John. Let

* Murray.   † Ibid.

them copy them without injuring them, whatever may be necessary for their purpose, and let them be equally seen and used by the children of my brother Carbry as by themselves, . . . and I request the children of Carbry to instruct their children." About a mile east of the castle of the O'Clerys are the remains of Kilbarron Church, said to have been founded by St Collum-Cille,* from which the parish takes its name. The tourist may now proceed northwards to Coolmore, where there is a retired bathing-place, and return by a different road to Ballyshannon.

III. Excursion to Pettigo and Lough Derg.

Ballyshannon is a good point from whence to visit Lough Derg, the scene of the celebrated penitential retreat known by the name of St Patrick's Purgatory. The distance to Pettigo is seventeen miles. Leaving Ballyshannon, the road runs eastward along the north bank of the Erne, passing Cliff Castle, Rockfield House, Belleek, where the road begins to take a north-eastern direction, and to afford beautiful and rapidly changing views to the south, over Lough Erne. About two miles from

* Variously written Columba, Columb, Columkille, and Collum-Cille in the Irish MSS.

Belleek is Keenahan Lough, on the left, and on the opposite side of the road Magheramenagh Castle; and a little farther on are a glebe-house, prettily situated, and Lough Scolban, on the left, while on the right, as you proceed, the extensive grounds of Castlecaldwell stretch away to the edge of Lough Erne. The road now hugs the shore of this beautiful lake, which, though from most points of view it appears encumbered with islands, here spreads out into a sea. The expanse, however, is soon broken by Boa, the largest of Lough Erne's numerous islands. Crossing the Waterfoot river, where there is a handsome residence (H. W. Barton, Esq.) of the same name, you once more pass into the county of Donegal, and after two miles more, you arrive at Pettigo, (*Inn:* Hamilton's,) on the river Termon, "in the parish of Templecarne, near the glebe-house of which are the ruins of Termon Magrath, a strong keep, with circular towers at the angles, said to have been the residence of Myler Magrath, the first Protestant bishop of Clogher."* Pettigo is situated on the southern border of a wild and desolate mountain region, in which, between four and five miles to the north, lies Lough Derg. The Rev. Cæsar Otway, in a sketch of an excursion made by him to this famous lough, has given a graphic

* Murray.

description of the approach to it :—" The road from the village of Pettigo, leading towards Lough Derg, runs along a river tumbling over rocks ; and then, after proceeding for a time over a boggy valley, you ascend into a dreary and mountainous tract, extremely ugly in itself, but from which you have a fine view indeed of the greatest part of the upper lake of Lough Erne, with its many elevated islands, and all its hilly shores. . . . . . I had at length, after travelling about three miles, arrived where the road is discontinued, and, by the direction of my guide, ascended a mountain path that brought me through a wretched village, and led to the top of a hill. Here my boy (guide) left me, and went to look for the man who was to ferry us to Purgatory, and on the ridge where I stood I had leisure to look around. To the south-west lay Lough Erne, with all its isles and cultivated shores ; to the north-west Lough Derg, and truly, never did I mark such a contrast. Lough Derg under my feet ; the lake, the shore, the mountains, the accompaniments of all sorts presented the very landscape of desolation— its waters expanding in Highland solitude, amidst a wide waste of moors, without one green spot to refresh the eye, without a house or tree, all mournful in the brown hue of its far-stretching bogs, and the gray uniformity of its rocks ; the surrounding mountains, even, partook of the sombre character of the place ; their forms without grandeur, their ranges continuous, and without elevation. The lake was certainly as fine as rocky shores and numerous islands could make it, but it was encompassed with such dreariness . . . . . I said to myself, 'I am already in Purgatory.' A person who had never seen the picture that was now under my eye, who had read of a place consecrated to the devotion of ages, might imagine that St Patrick's Purgatory, secluded in its sacred island, would have all the venerable and Gothic accompaniments of olden time; and its ivied towers and belfried steeples; its carved windows and cloistered arches; its long, dark aisles and fretted vaults, would have risen out of the water, rivalling Iona or Lindesfarne ; but nothing of the sort was to be seen."* In the same place Mr Otway relates that, in 1632, " the state ordered Sir James Balfour and Sir William Stewart to seize unto his Majesty's use this island of Purgatory ; and accordingly we find that Sir William proceeds to the island, and reports that he found an abbot and forty friars, and that there was a daily resort of four hundred and fifty pilgrims, who paid eightpence each for admission to the island. Sir William further informs the Privy Council, that in

* Sketches in Donegal, Letter iv.

order to hinder the seduced people from going any longer to this stronghold of Purgatory, and wholly to take away the abuse hereafter, he had directed the whole to be defaced and utterly demolished; therefore the walls, works, foundations, vaults, &c., he ordered to be rooted up, also the place called St Patrick's bed, and the stone on which he knelt. These and all other superstitious relics he ordered to be thrown into the lough; and he made James M'Grath, the owner of the island, to enter into recognisances that he should not in future permit the entrance of Jesuits, friars, nuns, or any other superstitious order of Popery, to enter therein."

It would appear that consequent upon this thorough "rooting up" by Sir William, the *locale* of the station was changed to the present Station Island, which is smaller and farther removed from the shore. The friars, who were the object of his wrath, were the family of a venerable Augustinian monastery, founded here by St Dabheog,* a disciple of St Patrick. In the martyrology of Donegal we read, under the 1st of January, the following notice of Lough Derg: "At the eastern extremity of that lake are Patrick's Purgatory and Dabheog's Island; there is also a monastery in which there were canons at the eastern extremity of the same lake. . . There

---

* Usually pronounced, Davoc.

E

are five beds of hard penance there, round which the
pilgrims go—the bed of Patrick, of Columbkille, of
Brigid, of Adamnan, of Dabheog."* The lake is
about six miles from north to south, and four miles
from west to east. The Station Island is a narrow
strip of rock, wholly occupied with buildings of the
most unpretending character. It is about half a
mile from the shore, and there is a ferry-boat, which
pays a handsome sum to the lord of the soil for the
exclusive privilege of taking the pilgrims to and
from the island. The station is open only from the

* Martyrology of Donegal, App. to Introd., xl. The Martyrology
of Donegal, or, A Calendar of the Saints of Ireland, was published
last year (1864) by the Irish Archæological and Celtic Society, Dublin. This work was compiled by Brother Michael O'Clery, chief of
the celebrated antiquaries, known by the name of the Four Masters.
The present beautiful edition contains the original text and a translation, the joint work of the Rev. J. H. Todd, T.C.D., and the Rev.
H. Reeves, gentlemen to whom the Irish literature of our age is
deeply indebted. The Martyrology was finished at the convent of
Donegal on the 19th of April 1630. " It is a compilation," writes
Mr Todd, "made by a scholar peculiarly well qualified for the task;
who had access to all the original authorities then extant in the Irish
language, the matter of which he has transferred either in whole or
in part into the present work, quoting in almost every instance
the sources from which he drew his information." (Ibid., p. xiii.)
" O'Clery was assisted by his companions in the great work of the
Annals of the Four Masters. The work, therefore, possesses no
small authority, as the compilation of scholars of the greatest
eminence, who have condensed into its pages the substance of original records, some of them no longer extant, and all requiring the
highest order of Celtic learning to read and interpret them correctly.
It is, in fact, a manual of great practical utility, and may be considered
as a synopsis of the particular branch of historical literature to which
it relates." (Ibid., p. xxi.)

1st of June to the 15th of August, the number of penitents each season varying from ten to fifteen thousand.

It has been justly observed by the writer of "Murray's Handbook," that it is foreign to the scope of such a work to describe the details of religious ceremonies. However, as it is there stated, on the authority of another, that the penitents are made to pass on their bare knees over hard and pointed rocks, the present writer, who has had the very best opportunities of knowing the exact truth in the matter, thinks it right to state that no such observance is practised on the island. The sum total of the austerities of the three days' "retreat" at Lough Derg consists in fasting on bread and water, (which the pilgrims, by a beautiful fiction, call wine,) and keeping vigil for one whole night in the church. The essential work of the "station" here is to withdraw from all temporal affairs, to make three days' spiritual recollection, ending in a confession.

From Pettigo there is a road direct to Donegal, but the tourist had better take the road to Ballintra, in order that he may have an opportunity of seeing the Pullens at Brownhall. Both roads traverse a wild and desolate highland moor, with only a small tarn here and there to break the dreary monotony. About fourteen miles from Pettigo, you arrive at

Brownhall, the residence of J. Hamilton, Esq., where the lover of scenery will find something to interest him. The chief object of interest is the Pullens. This is a deep ravine, darkly shaded with wood, through which a mountain torrent leaps joyously, then suddenly plunges through a cleft in the rock of from thirty to forty feet in depth, making here and there an acute angle, now disappearing under some cavernous arch, then reappearing beyond, and thus pursues its uneven way until about half a mile farther down, it comes out in placid stream, suddenly to lose itself again in a dark chasm some sixty feet deep, from which it emerges under a natural bridge, and courses on in a straight line to Ballintra, whither the tourist will be sure quickly to follow. Here, at the Catholic chapel, a building solid and graceful, he joins our main route, about seven miles from Ballyshannon.

FROM BALLYSHANNON TO DONEGAL,

The road traverses for the first five or six miles a bare, uninteresting upland. About midway, the geologist will observe the striking development of the mountain limestone near Ballintra, where there is nothing to detain the tourist, save the Pullens at Brownhall, already noticed. Two miles farther on

is Coxtown, the residence of A. Hamilton, Esq., beyond which you drop into the village of Laghy,
where the scenery begins to be diversified with some
bits of pretty landscape. Leaving on the left Belle
Isle, the residence of A. H. Foster, Esq., and a little
farther on, St Ernans, the seat of J. Hamilton, Esq.,
beautifully situated at the mouth of Donegal harbour, on an island connected by a causeway with
the mainland, you arrive at

DONEGAL.

[*Hotel:* Dillon's.]

Distances.—Mountcharles, 4 miles; Killybegs, 17;
Carrick, 24; Lough Eske, $4\frac{1}{2}$; Barnesmore Gap, 7;
Stranorlar, 17; Strabane, 30; Glenties, 15; Ardara,
$17\frac{1}{2}$; Ballyshannon, $13\frac{1}{2}$; Sligo, 39.

The town, from which the county takes its name,
occupies a beautiful situation at the head of the
bay of the same name. It consists of some 1550
inhabitants. The houses occupying the three sides
of a central triangle, called the Diamond, with its
outlets, are generally well built. As the harbour is
for the most part shallow and beset with numerous
shoals, the town is not important as a port, the
shipping trade being confined almost exclusively to
a corn trade carried on by A. MacAloone, Esq. "The

Protestant church is in the principal square, and
has a pretty spire and a hideous body. A dissent-
ing congregation have lately erected a chapel, which
might be admired, had the builder not committed
the unpardonable error of blocking up the best view
of the old castle."[*]

Donegal was incorporated into a borough by
charter of James I., February 27, 1612, the corpo-
ration consisting of Portreeve, twelve free burgesses,
and an unlimited number of freemen. It returned
two members to the Irish Parliament till it was disfranchised by the Union, for which the Earl of Arran
and Viscount Sudley took £15,000 as compensation.
There is a sulphurous spa, but little frequented, in
the neighbourhood.

But Donegal—*Dun-nan-Gal,* the Fort of the
Stranger—is classic ground for the antiquary. The
tourist will pay a visit to the site of the *Abbey,*
which is within five minutes' walk of the hotel.
Its situation at the head of the bay is exquisitely
beautiful. The long narrow harbour, placid as a
lake, flanked on either side by grassy slopes, diversified with many-tinted woods, and here and there
a steep incline green to the water's edge, all make
up a landscape of surpassing loveliness. The remains of the old monastery are lamentably scanty.

[*] Murray.

Enough, however, remains of the chapel to enable one to determine that it was a large cruciform building, with probably a central tower, and very graceful windows. Of the cloisters, too, there is left a memorial of thirteen arches, which, with their supporting couplets of pillars, yet retain evidences of great beauty and variety of design, and admirable execution. They are of the small size common in examples of Irish monastic architecture. But though the material lineaments of this building are so sadly effaced, it has left an impress on Irish history indelible as that history itself. It was a Franciscan monastery, founded in the year 1474, by Nuala O'Connor, the pious wife of Hugh Roe O'Donnell. Nuala dying before it was finished, the second wife of O'Donnell, Fingalla, daughter of O'Brien, king of Thomond, had the honour of completing it. It was richly endowed by O'Donnell;—indeed it seems to have been from the first specially favoured by that princely family, some of whom took the habit of St Francis, and many of whom lie buried there.

In 1505 Hugh O'Donnell built a castle in the immediate vicinity of this friary. Towards the end of the sixteenth century, during the reign of Hugh Dhu O'Donnell, in his youth a brave warrior, but now old and feeble, two English captains entered by sea from Sligo, fortified themselves at Ballyweel, a small island at the mouth of the harbour, and soon after succeeded in establishing themselves in the monastery, whence they pillaged the country round. They fled, however, at the approach of the young Hugh Roe O'Donnell after his escape from his long and dreary imprisonment in Dublin Castle, and the friars were reinstalled in their monastery.

But a dark day was coming on. While Hugh Roe was engaged in Connaught, the English won over his cousin and kinsman, the active Nial *Garv.* Nial, having first put the English in possession of the O'Donnell's castle at Lifford, next marched to Donegal with, besides his own followers, a body of 500 English from Dowcra, and seized the monastery, which he fortified for defence. The friars fled.*

---

* There is a curious account of the flight of the friars in a manuscript history, in Latin, in the possession of the Franciscans at Louvain, compiled by a Father Purcel. He says, " In the year 1600 we were in the convent of Donegal, forty brothers in community, and the divine offices for the night and the day were chanted with great solemnity. I myself had charge of the Sacristy, in which I had forty suits of vestments with all their appurtenances, and many of them were of cloth of gold and of silver, some were interwoven and ornamented with gold, all the rest were silk. There were eighteen silver chalices of large size, all gilt except two ; there were two ciboriums for the Most Holy Sacrament." Father Purcel then proceeds to tell that at the approach of the English the brothers fled away, and that ho himself carried with him this altar furniture in a boat, all which not long after fell into the hands of Oliver Lambert, the English governor of Connaught, who converted the chalices into profane uses, and destroyed the vestments. After the peace made between Roderick O'Donnell and the king of England, the former set about

Hugh Roe hastened to Donegal, and laid siege to the monastery occupied by his false cousin. Nial was brave, and resisted to the last, so that Hugh Roe had nothing for it but to sit down before the monastery and invest it. On the night of the 19th September a fire broke out in the building. Hugh Roe seized the occasion for an assault. The men on both sides fought like lions. All through that night did the fierce struggle last, the conflagration adding a ghastly horror to the wild work of death, till at length in the early morning, Nial with the survivors of the garrison retreated, keeping along the strand, under cover of a ship in the harbour, and took refuge in the neighbouring abbey at Magherabeg. Donegal monastery never recovered from the ruin of that night. After some years, when the terrible war between Hugh Roe and the English had come to an end, the friars began to creep out from their hiding places, and by degrees establish themselves in some cottages which they built among the ruins of their late home. In these cottages—the primitive form of monastery—was written the chro-

rebuilding the monastery, but, understanding that his life was in danger, he fled with O'Neil to Flanders, and thus the work was not proceeded with. Ware says that this convent was famous for a well-stored library, which O'Donovan conjectures was destroyed in the conflagration of the 19th September 1601.—*Apud* O'Donovan's edition of the Four Masters, introduction, p. xxix.

nicle known as the Annals of Donegal, or the Annals
of the Four Masters, which has given to this abbey
its special celebrity. "In whatever point of view,"
writes the late lamented Professor O'Curry, "we
regard these annals, they must awaken feelings of
deep interest and respect; not only as the largest
collection of national, civil, military, and family
history ever brought together, in this or perhaps
any other country, but also as the final winding-up
of the affairs of a people who had preserved their
nationality and independence for a space of over
two thousand years, till their complete overthrow
about the time at which this work was compiled.
It is no easy matter for an Irishman to suppress
feelings of deep emotion, when speaking of the compilers of this great work; and especially when he
considers the circumstances under which, and the
objects for which, it was undertaken. The chief of
these now-called Four Masters was Michael O'Cleary,
and his collaborators were Ferfessius O'Maelchonaire,
Peregrine or Cugory O'Dubhghennain, men of consummate learning in the antiquities of the country,
and of approved faith, and to these subsequently
was added the co-operation of other distinguished
antiquarians."* Michael O'Cleary, the author of many
learned works on Irish subjects, appears to have

* Lecture vii., O'Curry's Lectures.

been born in Kilbarron near Ballyshannon, in the county of Donegal, sometime about the year 1580. He was descended from a family of hereditary scholars, lay and ecclesiastical, and received, we may presume, the rudiments of his education at the place of his birth. In course of time he entered the Franciscan order : we don't know exactly the date. "The grand object of the Four Masters is to give chronological dates, and with the exceptions above, nothing can be more accurate. The years of foundations, and destructions of churches and castles, the obituaries of remarkable persons, the inaugurations of kings, the battles of chiefs, the contests of clans, the ages of bards, abbots, bishops, &c., are given with a meagre fidelity which leaves nothing to be wished for but some details of manners, which are the grand desideratum in the chronicles of the British Islands." *
"With all that Doctor O'Connor has so judiciously said here, I fully agree," observes O'Curry. "A book consisting of 11,000 quarto pages, beginning with the year of the world 2242, ending with the year of our Lord's incarnation 1616, thus covering the immense space of 4500 years of a nation's history, must be dry and meagre of detail in some, if not in all parts of it. And although the learned compilers

* Dr O'Connor's Catalogue of Stowe MSS., p. 133, cit. by O'Curry, Lecture vii.

had at their disposal, or within their reach, an immense mass of historic details, still the circumstances under which they wrote were so unfavourable, that they appear to have exercised a sound discretion, and one consistent with the economy of time and of their resources, when they left the details of our very early history in the safe-keeping of such ancient original records as from remote ages preserved them, and collected as much as they could make room for of the events of more modern times, in which they lived themselves . . . . . The last part of the annals was evidently intended to be a history." *

A short distance from the abbey stood, right on the brink of the beautiful Esk, the castle of Donegal, but here it is not given to the visitor to look upon the *debris* of the castle of the O'Donnells. The pile before him is what remains of "a beautiful Elizabethan building, combining defensive with domestic purposes,"† built by Sir Basil Brook out of the old castle which had been made over to him by royal grant in 1601. It is, however, a remarkable ruin. The visitor must view it from a short distance to catch the lines of its gabled tower, surmounted by a bartizan turret rising to a dizzy height. Within, the chief points of interest are a

* Lecture vii., O'Curry's Lectures.　　† Murray.

fine chamber containing a grand chimney-piece sculptured in good style with the arms of Brook and Leicester, and lighted by a splendid window. There are some fine stone mullions and arches, and a low room rudely vaulted with stones placed edge-ways.*

I. EXCURSION TO LOUGH ESK AND BARNESMORE.

It is an easy excursion from Donegal to Lough Esk, and the Gap of Barnesmore, a pass which every tourist in the Donegal Highlands ought to see. The road is up the valley of the Esk. Directly you leave the town the dark forms of the Croaghgorm (Bluestack) mountains begin to mass away to the left, and soon to approach your path. At the end of the third mile you are gladdened by the blue waters of Lough Esk, a basin some three and a half miles across, under an outlier of that fine range. The mountain border in great part rises with

---

* It may be right here to correct an error into which the writer of Murray's Handbook has been led, probably by Lewis's Top. Dict. He writes :—"In 1587 O'Donnell held his castle in defiance against the English Government, who, not having sufficient forces to send against him, captured it by stratagem. A vessel was sent to the coast laden with wine, the effects of which were too powerful for the chief, who had rashly accepted the hospitalities of the captain. He was bound, when drunk, and carried to Dublin Castle, from which, however, he eventually escaped," (p. 78.) The fact is, that it was not the chief, but his son, Hugh Roe, then a youth of fifteen, who was carried off from Rathmullen. The reader will find this interesting incident noticed at length under " Rathmullen."

abruptness sufficient to give the effect of precipice, yet holds enough of earth to nourish a coat of fresh-coloured mountain grasses, and though in one or two places it is rudely broken by the mountain torrents, there is at the lower extremity the pleasant greenness of easy slopes, amidst which reposes Esk House, (J. Brook, Esq.;) and at the upper extremity there is room for the demesne of Ardnamona, (G. C. Wray, Esq.,) with its picturesque clumps and fringes of trees. But in all this there is not that which makes a scene of soft beauty; for despite these pleasant accessories, the mountains are still the main characteristics and the striking feature of the landscape. On a small island near the southern extremity of the lake are the remains of a castle or keep built there by the O'Donnells, and said to have been used chiefly as a prison. In spite of the etymology of the word, for *Esk* means *fish*, neither the lake nor the river is at the present day remarkable for an abundance of fish; but the waters possess, they say, the richer property of pearl-producing—some pearls of great beauty having been found in them. He who is given to botanical pursuits will find in this neighbourhood a profitable field to explore. "*Polypodium phegopteris* and *Asplenium viride* grow near the waterfall at the lake."

Crossing the Lowreymore river the road brings

you soon into quite a different scene, the Gap of
Barnesmore. It is truly a noble pass of some three
or four miles, cutting right across a mountain range,
and shut in on either side by a threatening wall of
mountain,—that on the right, Croaghconnellagh,
rising to the height of 1724 feet, and that on the
left, Barnesmore, to the height of 1491 feet. The
steep escarpments at some points run out into beetling cliffs, at other points are furrowed by rents,
dark and ghastly, cut by the water-courses, which,
with a peculiarity not unusual to mountain torrents,
show a partiality for the steepest places, as if for
a headlong leap. The defile, though wild in the
extreme, does not, however, wear a look of utter
desolation, for there is a sufficiency of vegetation,
consisting of grass, and heath, chiefly of a brown
colour, but under the various conditions of weather
producing a rich variety of those beautiful hues
which can be caught only in mountain scenery.
"Oh, how I wished," writes the Rev. C. Otway,*
"even at the expense of a thorough wetting, to go
through this pass after a fall of rain,—to see hundreds of cataracts tumbling headlong on either side
—to hear the rush of the river, the roar of the
waterfalls, and moanings of the mountain blast—
realising the poet's description, when

* Sketches in Donegal.

'Red came the river down,
And loud and long the angry spirit of the waters shrieked.'"

At the further end of the defile, the watershed
(538 feet above the level of the sea) is reached,
near which is a spot, where, it is said, a man was
hanged not many years since for a murder committed
at this place.   A little farther on you will observe,
on an eminence on the left, a dark ruin of a castellated mansion built during James's wars, where, if
we are to believe the story told by Mr Otway, the
Huguenot historian Rapin compiled his voluminous
history.   On the right, close to the road, is Lough
Mourne, the source of the Mourne Beg river, which,
flowing eastward into Tyrone, passes on to unite its
waters with the Finn, at Lifford.   The surroundings
of Lough Mourne are of the most sombre and dreary
cast, but somewhat relieved of its desolateness by
some road-side cottages and patches of green fields.
The road from this point to Stranorlar is traced in
an excursion from that place to Donegal.

II. Excursion to Glenties.

From Donegal to Glenties the direct road lies
along the main route for some five miles, when it
strikes off to the right, passing Frasses Catholic
chapel, and dropping into the valley of the Eanymore and Eanybeg.   At the source of the Eanybeg

water, some five or six miles away, is a pretty dell, called Dysert, where are the grass-grown remains of an ancient chapel, and a well of St Collum Cille, and where many touching traditions of the saint are told. Right above Dysert rises the rugged peak of Carnaween, which has a *cromlech* on its summit, and commands a magnificent view of the north-western coast of Donegal and the mountains away to the east and south. Crossing the Eanybeg bridge, the road ascends a long and tedious hill, with the huge mass of Binbane rising steeply on the right. Looking back, the traveller gets superb views from every point of the road, and, when the watershed is reached, his course is enlivened by constantly shifting panoramas of mountains as he journeys over these heathy heights, from which he descends into the valley of the Owentucker, a torrent which accompanies him down its rocky channel as far as Kilrain, where he joins the main route between Ardara and Glenties.

DONEGAL TO KILLYBEGS.

The route now coasts westwards along the Bay of Donegal. Crossing the Esk, the road passes through smiling fields and gardens, dotted with comfortable cottages, and at the end of the first mile descends upon a beautiful inlet of the sea, which is shallow, and therefore seen to best advantage at high water, when it looks an extensive inland lake, with low banks, green to the water's edge. Farther on, the road begins to ascend, and you slowly wind your way up to "Mountcharles, a large village, built on the side of a steep hill." *   Under the town is the Hall, a handsome residence belonging to the Marquis of Conyngham, and commanding a view to the south over an arm of Donegal Bay and the uplands of Tirhugh, and the mountains behind Lough Melvin. Two miles farther down is Salt Hill, (R. Russell, Esq.,) occupying a charming situation at the edge of the coast, which is here flat and highly cultivated.

Arrived at the top of the hill above Mount-charles, the view is fine, to whatever point of the compass you turn your eyes. You can survey, from a near point of view, Donegal Bay, which you have already seen from the high beaches of Bundoran and Kilbarron. In front of you is a mountain chain rising out of the sea to the west, which, beginning with Cronnarad, runs eastward, forming with Mulmussog, Binbane, Silver Hill, and Bluestack a semicircle terminating in Barnesmore. Looking back, you get a fine view of the Benbulben and Truskmore ranges

* Murray.

to the south, and if the atmosphere is clear, you are able to trace the coast-line of the Connaught shores, far away to the south-west. Two or three miles to the right is Drumkeelin, the locality in which were found those fossil remains that have made the parish of Inver familiar to every student of geology and Irish archæology. Your route now lies down hill, giving off, to the right, a road to Glenties, traced under the excursion from Donegal to that place, to Inver, where a church with a pretty spire, and two handsome residences, (Mr Sinclair's, and the Rev. Mr Carr's,) standing on the opposite sides of a river, with a few white cottages, all half hidden among trees, variously grouped, make a charming picture. The river is the Eanybeg, which rises some ten miles away to the right, among the steeps of Silver Hill. There is good sport for the angler on this river, when there is a "fresh," or half flood, late in the season. Half a mile up the river is a bit of romantic scenery at Bony-Glen. Crossing Inver bridge, a little beyond which a road is given off to Ardara, the route is over rather uneven ground; but, "notwithstanding the tediousness of those hilly roads, the tourist will rarely find the time hang heavy; for the views of the Donegal mountains are superb."[*]
At the summit of this long stretch of rising ground is

* Murray.

"DUNKANEELY, a decayed-looking village of one street, from which the traveller will not be loath to emerge."* Pursuing your road down a slope of good land, you pass the church and comfortable parsonage (Rev. Mr Beaty) of Killaghtee.

Here the tourist may make a detour to explore St John's Point, a singular stretch of land, hardly a mile in mean width, running some seven miles into the sea in a south-westerly direction. Following the road branching off from the main route below Killaghtee, the tourist has on his right MacSwyne's Bay, on the shore of which, out at the water's edge, at a place called Castle-point, are the remains—reduced to a heap of the merest rubbish—of the old castle of the MacSwynes of Banagh, and a short distance beyond, a little nearer to the road, are the remains of an old church. Some two or three miles farther down the Point, as it is usually called in the district, is the grass-grown ruin of an old abbey or church, at a place called Ballysaggart—Priest's Town. Still farther down is a coast-guard station, and at the extreme end a lighthouse, standing ninety-seven feet above the sea.

You must now retrace your steps to join the Killybegs road, which leads by Bruckless, where there are a couple of pretty residences, and, a little

* Murray.

beyond, the Catholic chapel, occupying an elevation on the east bank of the Carker river, which here dives into a ravine made picturesque by a dark wood, from which a pillar of blue smoke may be seen ascending on a quiet afternoon. Crossing the Carker at the Oiley Bridge there is a good mile of rising ground patched with furze and brown grasses, and then you "descend upon the most charming of landlocked bays," on one side of which, completely sheltered from the storms, is

KILLYBEGS, "a clean, pleasant, little seaport, which, without any pretensions to the dignity of a watering-place, will, as far as situation goes, well repay a visit."* There are two hotels—Coane's and Rodgers's.

Distances.—Kilcar, 6½ miles ; Carrick, 9 miles ; Slieve League, 12 miles ; Glen, 16½ miles ; Malinmore, 17 miles ; Ardara, 10 miles ; Glenties, 16 miles.

It is built literally on the edge of the sea. The White House (G. V. Wilson, Esq.) rises out of the water, and on the opposite side of the road are schools, remarkable for their pretty architecture. The Catholic chapel is a beautiful building, commanding a fine view over the town and harbour, and adjoining it is the neat residence of the parish priest (the Rev. Mr Stephens.) The harbour is com-

* Murray.

pletely secured.   It opens to the south by a narrow entrance, at which is a lighthouse, on an insulated rock, call the Rotten Island.   The shore all round the bay is abrupt and craggy, but there is enough of green to redeem it from wildness.   The visitor should take an hour's boating in the bay for sake of the views, especially of the town—which seems to float on the tide—and its rocky background.   A boat may be had at Coane's well-appointed hotel.

Killybegs, anciently called *Calla-beaga,** or Na-Calla, as it is still designated by the Irish-speaking population, possesses some interest for the antiquary.   Beside the glebe-house, on the western shore of the bay, are the grass-grown remains of a castle and a Franciscan friary, built by the Mac-Swiney of Banagh, on the site of which there seems to have been a Catholic chapel down to comparatively late times, under the patronage of St Catherine.

The town was incorporated by royal charter in the thirteenth year of the reign of James I. into a borough with the titles of "provost, free burgesses, and commonalty of Callebegg," and returned two members to the Irish parliament, down to the Union, when it was disfranchised—Henry, Earl of

---

* Little Churches.

Conyngham, pocketing the whole of the compensation, £15,000.

"The tourist should now take a car, there being no other public conveyance, to explore the district beyond Killybegs, which, as far as scenery goes, is equal to anything in Ireland, and deserves to be thoroughly well known." * Starting from Killybegs you begin at once to labour against a steep ascent, from the slope of which, looking back, you get a view which, for variety of incident, is rarely equalled. The little town under your feet with its gigantic barrier of crags standing up behind it, the placid basin, with its translucent waters and brim of rock and pasture, interwoven in every conceivable figure, all looking clean and bright even in murky weather, and the distant hills cutting the horizon into long and graceful lines, are the characteristics of the scene. After the first mile, you suddenly drop upon a maritime dell with a singularly bold background. There is a broad strip of yellow strand, from which Fintra Bay spreads out to the south-west, and upon the beach is Fintra House, (R. Hamilton, Esq.,) embosomed in trees, while close behind tower the dark steeps of Cronnarad. The road now keeps along the coast, which slopes rapidly to the sea, having still the ridge of

* Murray.

Cronnarad, gray and rugged, on the right, and commanding seaward a magnificent view of Donegal Bay with its southern coast-line from the sandhills of Bundoran, backed by the Benbulben and Truskmore ranges, the distant mountains of Erris and Tyrawley. The tourist should note the phenomena of colour on those distant hills. As he proceeds he will be much struck with the cleanliness and comfort of the cottages that line the road, due in great measure to Mr Wilson, the able and humane manager of Mr Murray Stewart's estate in this district.

At the fifth mile the direct road bends inland to Kilcar, but the tourist had better go by the less-frequented one which skirts the base of Muckross (916 feet) on the side next the sea, and affords bits of coast scenery that will more than repay the inconvenience of the detour. Perched high on what is more a cliff than a hillside are numerous cottages, the airy tenements of fishermen, who, in addition to the precarious livelihood drawn from the deep, manage to raise potatoes among the rocks. Arrived at a spot where there is a school-house standing by itself on the roadside, the tourist will have no difficulty in finding among the houses in the neighbourhood some one to guide him to the caves which open on the sea at the end of Muckross Point.

These are a series of marine chambers, each consisting of the three sides of a square cut clean out of
the living rock, and a flat roof of immense flags
admirably jointed together. There is an enormous
cube of rock in the largest of these caves called the
Market House. They are not accessible at the
higher stages of the tide, but it is worth while to
wait till the water has receded sufficiently to allow
one to explore them. Above, on the western extremity of this bit of headland, is shown a heap of
stones, said to be the remains of an old castle,
which, judging from the traditions, as well as from
the incidents of the situation, was probably one of
those Cyclopean towers of the Pagan period, so
common in the west and south of Ireland. Looking towards Carrigan Head, the western extremity
of Slieve League, there is a noble vista of precipices standing as pillars at the entrances into
Tawney and Teelin Bays. If the day is not unusu-
ally fine, the visitor should spend half-an-hour on
the strand under the school-house to observe the
majestic roll of the waves, which, under most conditions of weather, attain here a volume greater
than anywhere else all round this stormy coast.
He cannot fail to be struck with the position of
the school-house built *into* the abrupt acclivity of
the mountain. The school-boy when he leaves the

door sees below him a line of awful precipices, under which the Atlantic thunders unceasingly. Above him he sees the hardly less awful Muckross, so steep that the unaccustomed visitor cannot look up without a sensation of uneasiness lest he might fall back into the sea. Along this mountain side, gray with rocks threatening every moment to come down —stones not unfrequently do descend, acquiring in the fall a momentum equal to a cannon-shot—the road cuts its way, touching at two or three points on the very verge of precipices that take one's breath away, and quitting this dizzy course falls into a short fiord, called Tawney Bay, the western side of which is very precipitous, but crowned with clusters of cottages and cultivated patches of ground, presenting almost every possible geometrical combination of figure.

About half a mile above the head of the bay is

KILCAR, "a romantic village on the slope of a hill, at the foot of which is the church and a brawling mountain torrent, forming altogether a charming picture."* The Catholic chapel, neatly railed off the street, with the hospitable dwelling of the parish priest (Rev. H. O'Donnell) adjoining, is the most

---

* Murray, p. 83.

striking architectural feature of the place. On the hillside above the church are the remains of an old abbey.

The road to Carrick keeps the valley of the Bally-duff river for a good mile, and then crossing this stream ascends a slope of moorland, and again descending, shows you, nestling in the bosom of the giant Slieve League,

CARRICK, a small village situated on the bank of the Teelin river, about a mile above Teelin Bay.

Distances.—Glen, 6 miles; Malinmore, 7 miles; Ardara, 14 miles; Glenties, 20 miles.

"The tourist should make Carrick his head-quarters, at the pleasant little hotel built by Mr Connolly, M.P., where he will find great cleanliness and civility, with peculiar advantages for explor-ing a district teeming with coast and mountain beauty."* The lover of cliff scenery will have high holiday in this district. The writer of Murray's Handbook truly remarks that "the twenty miles from Teelin Bay to Loughros Bay is, as far as coast scenery goes, not to be excelled by any locality in Great Britain."†

* Murray.
† The visitor will observe that the line of coast alluded to is nearly twice twenty miles.

I. Excursion to Slieve League.

The tourist should tell his guide to lead him first to Carrigan Head. The road holds an even tenor on the left bank of the Teelin river, and then alongside the estuary of the same name. Teelin Bay is perfect in that peculiar beauty which belongs to landscape, of which all the lines of the picture are sharp, and every feature striking. In this land-locked little bay, with all its bold surroundings, you have views in rich abundance, which, if you have a turn for drawing, you will be tempted to sit down and sketch. Conspicuous amongst the cottages (which are pretty numerous) on the right bank is the glebe-house, (Rev. E. Labatt,) and down at the very gate of the harbour is a coast-guard station. As the tourist pursues his pleasant road, he will notice the heaps of bog iron-ore, which is found in large quantities in the elevated moors inland, and taken to Teelin for shipment. At the end of the third mile he takes a path to the right, which will lead him over the hill to the old martello signal-tower, whence he may begin to explore the magnificent precipices of Carrigan Head, a truly noble pier, 745 feet high, terminating in Slieve League at its southern end. On the mind susceptible in the least degree of the sublime, the impression produced by these precipices is intensely " sensational."

A word about the visitor of weak nerve, and unaccustomed to cliff scenery. To such a one coming close to the verge of these steeps, suddenly every object, except the immense expanse of ocean far below, and the empty space of sky before him and above him, goes out of his sight, and he feels as if the ground had by some magical influence shot back from under his feet, leaving him poised in mid-air, and this awful feeling may at once grow into one of helpless terror. Often one thrown into some such panic by the presence of an abyss is made miserable by the well-meant encouragements of others of his party. Encouragement is a necessary remedy, but it ought not to be accompanied with banter, which only·serves to irritate the mind more and more; nor by vehemence of argument, because the will is for the moment beyond the dominion of the reason. The best course is to let the person so affected rest a while on the lesser elevations, until the eye has been somewhat familiarised with the scenery, and has learned to measure steadily all its lines. When the visitor can look calmly on the spot where he plants his foot, and feels the ground solid under him, it is a sign that he has recovered the even balance of his faculties; he may then proceed, and those sensations which before were panic or terror, become the most elevating and delicious of excitements, surpassing anything that the finest efforts of the stage could produce.

From Carrigan Head the cliff curves slightly inward, making a small bay, called Bunglass. Ascending a short stretch of hill, you suddenly find yourself on the verge of Bunglass precipices, " where a view of singular magnificence bursts upon you—a view that, of its kind, is probably unequalled in the British Isles. The lofty mountain of Slieve League gives, on the land side, no promise of the magnificence that it presents from the sea, being in front a mural precipice of nearly 2000 feet in height, descending to the water's edge in one superb escarpment—

> ' Around
> Whose cavern'd base the whirlpools and the waves,
> Bursting and eddying irresistibly,
> Rage and resound for ever.' "*

The place where you stand is called the *Awark-Mor*, that is, the Great View. And it is in very truth a great view. As you stand at the end of a curve, a great portion of the face of the cliff is brought within your ken. At first the extraordinary altitude of the cliffs, descending sheer to the ocean, produces a sense that so absorbs one as to

* Shelley, cit. *apud* Murray.

leave no room for other impressions. But as by degrees the eye comes to take in the picture in detail,
a play of line and colour in wonderful combination
enchants the spectator. All round the sweep of
precipice there is a variety and richness of colour.
The hues of the different strata of rocks, the stains
of metals, the various tints of clays and mosses,—in
short, every colour in the rainbow, and every variety
of shade, come out before you in the sunshine—a
magnificent mosaic-work, beside which the noblest
efforts of human art sink into veriest miniature;
and then, the depths below supplying this wonderful
crescent with a translucent floor of blue, dark almost
to blackness, and the line of precipices beyond breaking, as they recede, into abutments, and towers, and
aerial tableaux, all go to make up the foreground of
the *Awark-Mor*. Somewhat to the right, not many
feet below the edge, is a dark dint in the face of the
precipice called the Eagle's Nest, a fit abode truly
for the royal bird.

To enjoy the scenery well, the visitor should
ascend by a path from Bunglass along the verge of
the precipice the whole way up to the top of the
mountain. On approaching the summit line he will
find that the mountain narrows to an edge, called
the One Man's Path, from the circumstance that
they who are bold enough to tread it must pass in

single file over the sharp ridge. On the land side an escarpment, not indeed vertical, but steep enough to seem so from above, descends more than a thousand feet to the brink of a small tarn ; while, on the side facing the sea, the precipices descend to from 1300 to 1800 feet, literally straight as a wall, to the ocean. A narrow footway, high in the air, with both these awful abysses yawning on either side, is the One Man's Path, which, in the language and imagination of the people of the district, is the special characteristic of Slieve League, a distinction that it surely merits. The writer, while he agrees with the observation in Murray's Handbook as to the absence of any real danger of destruction from this path, would be sorry to press any visitor of weak nerve to venture on a dizzy ledge which abounds in awful incident of the kind that had nearly proved fatal to Lady Staunton, who, says the story-teller of the Heart of Mid-Lothian, "was an admirer of the beauties of nature, a taste which compensates many evils to those who happen to enjoy it, appeared to feel an interest and energy while in the open air, and traversing the mountain landscapes with the two boys, whose ears she delighted with stories of what she had seen in other countries, and what she had to show them at Willingham Manor." One day " she walked five long miles, and over rough ground," to see a fine cascade in the hills ; and "the scene, when she reached it, amply rewarded the labour of the walk." The view of the shoot, however, was broken by a jutting rock. " Those who love nature always desire to penetrate into its utmost recesses, and Lady Staunton asked David whether there was not some mode of gaining a view of the abyss at the foot of the fall. He said that he knew a station, on a shelf on the further side of the intercepting rock, from which the whole waterfall was visible, but that the road to it was steep, slippery, and dangerous. Bent, however, on gratifying her curiosity, she desired him to lead the way ; and accordingly he did so, over crag and stone, anxiously pointing out to her the resting-places where she ought to step ; for their mode of advancing soon ceased to be walking, and became scrambling. In this manner, clinging like sea-birds to the face of the rock, they were enabled, at length, to turn round it, and came full in front of the fall, which here had a tremendous aspect, boiling, roaring, and thundering with unceasing din into a black caldron, a hundred feet at least below them, which resembled the crater of a volcano. The noise, the dashing of the waters, which gave an unsteady appearance to all around them, the trembling, even, of the huge crag on which they stood, the precari-

G

ousness of their footing—for there was scarce room for them to stand on the shelf of rock which they had thus attained—had so powerful an effect on the senses and imagination of Lady Staunton, that she called out to David she was falling, and would, in fact, have dropped from the crag had he not caught hold of her. The boy was bold and stout of his age, still he was but fourteen years old; and as his assistance gave no confidence to Lady Staunton, she felt her situation become really perilous. The chance was, that in the appalling novelty of the circumstances, he might have caught the infection of her panic, in which case it is likely that both must have perished. She now screamed with terror, though without hope of calling any one to her assistance. To her amazement, the scream was answered by a whistle from above, of a tone so clear and shrill, that it was heard even amid the noise of the waterfall." * Of course this whistle was the harbinger of sure relief.

The visitor who is afraid to trust himself on the One Man's Path may make a detour by Teelin, and gain the heights beyond by a gravelled path, on which one may ride to the top of the mountain. On the summit, within a short distance from the precipices, are the remains of an oratory and cell,

* The Heart of Mid-Lothian—Scott.

the hermitage, according to tradition, of a holy
recluse, named Hugh MacBracken. Here again
is another One Man's Path, not indeed so awful as
that which leads up from Bunglass, but still sufficiently tremendous to appal the unaccustomed visitor;
and yet it was, up till the making of the broad road
to Malinmore and Malinbeg, the great thoroughfare
between those coasts and the interior of the country.
As there is no danger, unless in the case of a very
strong wind blowing from the land, the tourist ought
to cross it to the other side, where this mountain cliff
attains its highest elevation, 1974 feet. The view
is worthy of this great maritime alp. Southwards,
you take in a noble horizon of mountains ranging
from Leitrim to the Stags of Broadhaven, and in
the dim distance are seen Nephin above Ballina,
and, when the atmosphere is peculiarly clear, Croagh-
Patrick above Westport. Looking inland you behold a sea of mountain tops receding in tumultuous
waves as far as the rounded head of Slieve Snaght,
and the sharp cone of Errigal. But, wondrous as is
this view, it is in the majesty of the cliff that the
scene is unrivalled. As one descends from the summit, on the farther side near the top, facing the sea,
are one or two groups of slender quadrilateral pillars
standing in singular isolation straight up from the
steeply escarped side, called *chimneys* by the country

people. Strange fancy! and they are beautifully taper-
ing chimneys to an edifice two thousand feet high,
and many miles round about. The tourist, cautiously
guarding his steps in the steep descent, should follow
his guide down to one of the "chimneys," not so much
with a view to inspect the example itself, as to gain
a new stand-point from which to see the precipices.
A quarry lately opened here shows this part of the
mountain to be formed of piles of thin small flags
of a beautiful white colour, thus proving what the
geologist would have seen at the first glance, that the
chimneys are portions of the formation of the precipice which have not yet wholly yielded to the
atmospheric action that has worn the rest into a slope.
And here observe how much there is in a name;
for Slieve League (or Liaga) means the Mountain
of Flags. Let the visitor now from this spot survey
the wondrous architecture of the great cliff. The
immense field of precipice down which he looks is
the result of a combination of projections, and
cavities, and ledges. Here a line of rock presenting
a sharp edge cut into a series of indentations; there
a recess running down the abyss like the hollow
in an enormous fluted column; there, again, is a
forest of projecting rocks assuming every form of
crest, and all marvellously checkered with seams of
stunted heath, dwarf shrubs, and peculiar grasses.

" The rocky summits, split and rent,
  Form'd turret, dome, or battlement,
  Or seem'd fantastically set
  With cupola or minaret,
  Wild crests as pagod ever deck'd,
  Or mosque of eastern architect." *

Far below, through the splintered crags, is a vista
of brightest green—a delicious carpet, soft-looking
as a palace park.

The range of precipices continues unbroken, but
gradually diminishing in elevation, on to Malinbeg,
(five miles;) and the views along this whole line will
amply repay the tourist for the fatigue of the walk
to Rossarell Point. At Malinbeg, where the sea
has cut a crescent into the lofty beach, is a belt of
beautiful strand, called Traban,† at the northern
extremity of which is a good example of fort or
"dun," called by the people of the locality, the
Doon, and in an adjoining creek there is a superb
monolith standing up out of the bright water.
From Malinbeg the tourist will proceed to Malinmore, two miles farther on, where he is sure to
find comfortable lodging at the house of Miss
Walker.

Should he desire to sail under the sea-cliffs of
Slieve League, an excursion which he should by all
means make, weather permitting, a boat and crew

* Scott.　　　　　　　† *Fair-strand.*

can be had at Teelin, which ought to be made the starting-point from whence to coast round all the way to Malinbeg. As so much has already been said about this range of precipices, there is no need of further observation as to the characteristics of the scenery, except to add that there are a few caverns which the boatmen will point out.

Many years ago, on the occasion of a great fair at Killybegs, a priest engaged two poets, famous in the locality, in a bardic contest, assigning to one for a theme Slieve League and its surroundings, and to the other the Muineagh, a hill rising behind Ardara. Each bard was put into a separate room for a stated time, after which he was led forth to recite his production before the general company. The result was two ballads of the true Homeric stamp, which are still remembered and sung in the recesses of Donegal. The poet of Slieve League sings of the slopes "running with honey as with mountain dew," and the "sweet milking of the kine," and the "frisking calves," and the "cliff-birds in playful debate about their lodging for the night," and "the hounds and wolf-dogs let loose at early dawn," and "the pleasant gatherings of the people," and "the lithe, fairy horsemen," and so on, with an inspiration full and rushing; then stopping short to contemplate the cliffs, he exclaims, "Here the monarchs of the ocean hold high festival below," while "the peak above sees many a wondrous sight."* And then, as if silenced by the vastness of the object, he abruptly breaks off his description. It is a noble idea that of the *noblesse* of the great deep holding tournament under these walls, and it may indeed be questioned, whether in the infinite range of ocean border all around the earth there be another spot so worthy of their distinguished companionship as that under Slieve League.

It is hardly necessary to observe, that many of the effects alluded to in these remarks are lost in cloudy or stormy weather; in which event, however, the visitor will be compensated by many other attributes brought out by the play of storm and cloud in this scenery, sublime under every aspect.

Many a " tale traditionary " hangs round Slieve League. Here is one related to the writer, while he rested on the steep declivity of the mountain on the Malinbeg side, by an intelligent young man, who accompanied the narrative with many handfuls of juicy bilberries, (found in great abundance at that spot about the middle of the month of August,) which he gathered while he told the story. One fine sunny day, early in September, a woman who

---

* The ballads are of course in the Irish language, and, like most ballads, would lose their charm by translation.

dwelt at the Teelin end of Slieve League, taking her child, a little girl of some ten months old, with her in her arms, came out into a field close by her cottage, where her husband with some others were making hay. She remained chatting to the labourers, and fondling her little darling till the child went to sleep; then the mother, making a soft bed for it of the newly saved hay warmed in the sun, laid it there, and watched by it, fondly raising the margin of the bed here, and smoothing it there. By and by, dinner hour came, and the mother was needed for a moment within. Looking at her child, and fidgeting once more with its bed, she soliloquised : " I'll not disturb the little *lanu*, she is sleeping so quietly ; she is sheltered from the air, and shaded from the sun. I'll just run into the house, and give the men milk for their dinner, and then I'll run back here. God keep you, my *lanu;* I'll be back in a minute." The woman went round to the house, and made haste to set the simple dinner before her humble household ; which done, she hastily left to return to the field. But just as she stepped outside the threshold, she came to a dead stand, and was speechless for a moment ; then uttering a wild cry, that made those within bound in their seats, darted from the door.

That shriek, in the quiet noontide air, when all

the peasants were in-doors at their mid-day meal, and not a murmur in the fields, penetrated far up and down the valley, and over the mountain side. In an instant every little elevation, whether of rock, or fence, or hillock, around the cottages, held a female in tragic attitude, or a man with head bare, and hands shading his eyes, or a promiscuous group gaining every instant fresh accessions of the very old, or the very young, all looking and pointing with a wild energy, but without clamour, towards one object. The cynosure of all this intense regard was a large dark eagle, holding an infant in his talons, circling slowly over the head of the mother of the child, who stood in the field below, with hands clasped convulsively, and her head and neck stretched upwards, as she followed with fixed gaze the gyrations of the bird of prey. Slowly still, and proudly did the eagle wind upwards his spiral way, till suddenly stopping, and balancing himself for a moment in mid-air, he shot towards the sea, and disappeared behind the cliff above the well-known eyry. The mother staggered and fell to the earth ; but after a long swoon returned to consciousness a helpless maniac. The highly-wrought feelings of the spectators—the astonishment, awe, and horror, hitherto hushed by the dread suspense and all-absorbing interest in the issue of the spectacle, now found utterance in a cry that seemed to make the mountain tremble to its foundations. Keeping up a wild and confused shout, the whole population rush to the cliff.

When the crowd had fairly congregated on the edge of the precipice, and the place had become a perfect Babel for the confusion of voices—ejaculatory prayers, frantic exclamations, anathemas, blessings, discussions, encouragements, warnings—all urged with a vehemence and volubility peculiar to the Irish character and language, the uproar was suddenly hushed by a fresh surprise. The eagle gliding out from beneath, made a rapid sweep over Bunglass, showing, as he gained a higher elevation, at each successive flap of his enormous wings, the child still coiled in his talons, as if by black ropes, and set out majestically in a horizontal line over the ocean.

The murmur was beginning to rise again from the crowd, when a certain man, venerable for his years and his virtues, and of high repute in the neighbourhood, invited all to fall on their knees and to pray to God, " for," said he, " we ought to know that God, and only God, can command the eagle." The crowd obeyed on the instant, and the old man continued, " Pray God that, if it be His holy will, He may rescue that helpless infant. Pray also to her who is herself a mother—the Great Mother—most loving, and most pure—pray that she may intercede with her Divine Son in behalf of the wretched mother who has been robbed before our eyes of her darling babe." They prayed fervently. Presently the old man again said : " Cease to look after the bird of evil, that you may pray without distraction ; leave me to watch him in his course, for God has gifted me with a power of sight beyond most men in Teelin." And they bent low in prayer, while above the murmur of their fervent orisons, the old man traced the onward course of the eagle. " Pray, pray old and young, for the bird does not return, but flies still farther over the ocean. Pray with all your soul, pious mothers, for the bird goes farther and farther away, as I know by its size growing smaller and smaller. Pray with all your strength, for the dark speck gets smaller and smaller. Pray with your whole hearts ; it is getting smaller and smaller. Pray, pray one and all, old and young ; he speck fades into bright air. O my God, does the hope fade from my eyes ! Pray ; I can see it still, though it is but a pin's point in the far off sky. Pray, and give thanks to God ; I see it still, it does not get smaller. Give thanks, give thanks, the bird returns, for the speck grows larger—yes, larger and darker. The eagle comes back in the same course in which it went out. It comes nearer still, and nearer. God has heard your prayers. The infant shall not be food for the eagles." The bird approached, glided in, dropped its unconscious burden in the eyry, and immediately flew away again. Directly the bird had flown out into space, a female, with eyes starting from their places, and hair flowing wildly back, disappeared over the precipice. The awe-struck crowd, who had seen the movement, held their breath. It was the mother; she had come to the cliff under the care of her relatives, and while the people were absorbed in prayer, had been lying prostrate on the earth, apparently unconscious of what was going on; but, with the instinct peculiar to such cases, she recognised the advancing eagle, and its immediate departure, and, quick as thought, ran to the edge of the precipice. The absence of reflection was her security. The rough face of the cliff became for her a ladder, every little crevice or wart serving for a step. She quickly descended, entirely unconscious of the awful surroundings, gained the eyry, which was spacious enough to admit her, took her child, and after kissing it with frantic passion, secured it in the train of her gown, drawn up over her shoulders, after a certain fashion peculiar to the humble matrons of the district, so as to form a bag on the back, and clomb the steep with the same unfaltering firmness and unconcern, as if it were a wall only a few feet from the ground. Great, of course, was the joy of the neighbours, and deep their gratitude to God as they returned home. The mother recovered her reason together with her child, who grew up to be a comely girl ; and, in due time, the mother of a daughter, " who," said my intelligent story-teller, " lived to be a very old woman, and was well known to the person who told me the story."

Another tale told to the writer on the same occasion deserves a place here, notwithstanding the likeness it bears to stories which the reader may have heard or read elsewhere.

Once upon a time, a poor " widow woman," crossing the mountain from Teelin to Malinbeg, found herself suddenly confronted by a wolf standing in her path. Afraid to fly, and afraid to advance, the terror-stricken matron stood still. The wolf also remained stationary, and thus both stood face to face ; till at length the woman, seeing nothing threatening in the demeanour of the animal, began to breathe freely, and to bestow on the dreaded monster a calmer and more searching scrutiny. She noted with infinite relief that the animal before her made no hostile demonstration whatever ; in fact, no movement of any kind, except to raise and drop one of its fore-feet, from time to time, and that its eyes had in them a certain tender expression without any of that fierceness always set down as characteristic of the wolf. And so, taking courage, she moved away, keeping still an eye on the animal, which regarded her with an imploring look while she passed, but when she had gone clear off, hobbled away on three legs. An idea suddenly occurred to the widow. Perhaps, thought she, this creature is suffering pain in one of its limbs, and has come out from its hiding-place to seek relief from me. She turned in the direction in which the wolf was going, and called after it, as one does after a favourite dog. The wolf stopped at once, and, turning round, approached the woman, till they were close to each other. The monster raised the wounded foot, and the woman probed it, and found a thorn buried in the extremity, where the wound had already begun to fester. Taking a strong pin from her shawl, she extracted the thorn, cleaned out the wound, and, leaving the wolf looking its gratitude, went on her way.

Next morning, there was confusion in the neighbourhood. Some who had been out early to see after their flocks and herds, found them missing. The hills had been swept of their live stock during the night. The alarm spread. A rigorous search is begun out of hand. Fleet-footed lads are despatched

in all directions. It was not long before the thief
was tracked to his place. In a garden enclosed by
walls of dry stones, the missing cattle were found
packed close together, while a wolf kept pacing up
and down before the gap or entrance to the garden,
howling and threatening fiercely when any one approached. Some of the shepherds not daring a single
encounter with the infuriate animal, took counsel to
stand together and attack the monster from a distance. Accordingly, after having collected a heap
of stones for the assault, they began to hurl them
against the wolf in thick showers; but the brave
sentinel, undaunted by these formidable missiles,
continued to trot up and down his beat, lashing his
sides with his tail, and through his bared teeth howling back defiance to the enemy. The threatening
shouts of the shepherds, mingling with the fierce
cries of the wolf, soon brought a crowd to the scene
of the encounter. The first to come was the " widow
woman," whose cottage adjoined the garden in which
the cattle were impounded. Awakened by the wild
uproar, she " put on her " hastily, and came round
by the garden wall. The wolf caught sight of her,
and forthwith his ears dropped, and he came to a
dead stand; the ferocious expression left his eyes
while he raised a fore-foot towards her. The woman,
recognising her acquaintance of yesterday, ap-

proached, and having examined the foot, found that
the wound was already healed. The wolf now led
the way into the garden through the open gap, the
woman following, and patting it on the neck as they
went. The beasts within crouched for fear, while
the wolf looked round, stretching his head now to
one side, and then to the other, pointing out the im-
prisoned cattle to the woman, with an expression in
its eyes that seemed to say : " Behold, these are my
return to you for your good office to me yesterday.
Accept them as a token of my gratitude to you:
they are yours." Then bending his neck to 'be
stroked again, the animal set off to the woods, leaving the shepherds in mute astonishment at these
later movements.

When the wolf had time to get into the recesses
of the woods, which at that period covered a great
portion of the mountain, the widow invited the
shepherds to take each his own, for she would not
have a reward paid out of the property of other
people, though she was poor, and sore in need of a
cow. And the owners, having heard and discussed
her strange story, returned home pondering, not without profit, on the deep impression which an act of
kindness will make even on so ferocious an animal
as a wolf.

But the story of Slieve League, and the one which

the passing visitor is most likely to hear, is, " The Story of the Spaniard," as they entitle it in the district.

The most prominent figure in the recent traditions of this locality is a certain priest, who, however, like every hero, real or imaginary, does not appear without secondary actors. Father Carr was always attended by his clerk, who was, as in duty bound, blindly obedient to his superior. He always rode a gray pony, which must have been an excellent specimen of the species, for tradition endows it with the faculty of intelligence. Happening on one occasion to be in Malinbeg, he accepted the invitation of an honest and well-to-do farmer of the place to spend the night at his house. He retired early, for the day had been one of unusual fatigue for him ; and then the clerk became the guest of the evening, a distinction that always pleased him. Seated in the midst of the simple family round the kitchen fire, he talked away in his best vein till it was late bedtime, when the younger members began to drop off one by one. But the clerk showed no desire to retire just then ; and it was, indeed, the kind of night on which one would appreciate a comfortable hearth, for the wind moaned dismally abroad, a storm having sprung up in the evening, and growing more violent every moment. He and the

" man of the house" talked on to a late hour. At last
the clerk heard his name called from the room occupied by the priest, which adjoined the kitchen. He
opened the door of the chamber, and found the priest
dressed. " Owen, my son," said the latter, " get the
pony saddled immediately, for we must cross Slieve
League as soon as we can ; and mind, don't make
any noise about it, for I wish to slip off as quietly
as possible." The clerk stood aghast at the command ; but, recovering himself in a moment, he promised prompt obedience, for there was that in the
priest's tone which was to him a sure indication that
remonstrance was useless.

The " man of the house" did all in his power to
dissuade the priest from going out. He reminded
him of the dangerous nature of the road along the
precipices of Slieve League, and over the One Man's
Path, and that on a night in which the wind was, to
use his own strong metaphor, " enough to blow the
horns off the cows." The priest interrupted him:
" Donal," said he, " it is moonlight, and even if it
were dark, I know the road well, and the pony
knows every inch of it. The One Man's Path is the
same to me as a broad road." The horse was brought
round to the door, and the priest, bidding a blessing
on the family, mounted.

" Owen, my son," began Father Carr when they

had advanced a little on their journey, " have you lost your tongue ? I fear you are a coward after all." " No, I'm no coward, and you, reverend father, know I'm no coward." " Good, Owen, good! I'm glad you are able to speak." " Well, father, it is strange, to say the least, that any one with right reason in his head should venture over Slieve League on a night when every human being ought to pray and give thanks to God for the shelter of a house." " Owen, the angels are abroad in stormy, as in calm, weather. Courage, my son, courage, the angels will guard us." The fear that had possessed the clerk for the moment arose from a sense of discomfort more than from any real terror ; it was therefore dispelled by this little speech, and his natural courage—for he was by nature fearless as a lion—coming back to him, he struck out into a bold, rapid walk.

Father Carr now apparently for the first time took note of the weather. He first directed his searching glance overhead, and the struggle between the moon, now high in the heavens, and the rushing clouds, was something worthy his rapt contemplation. It was glorious to see the shining orb, with edge sharp as a lance, plunge madly into the broken masses that flitted around it near and far, rushing forward in a whirling, tossing, aimless motion, and unwearied velocity, while it tore the flying sheets of cloud into a thousand rags, and sent the fragments floating away behind it. Below, the light accorded well with the wild fury of the elements,—now a long spell of doubtful shade darkening the headlands and the ocean into dim shadows, then a flood of bright moonshine suddenly revealing the waters in wild dance, and breaking the coast line of cliff and mountain into gigantic columns of jet and silver. The wind, which was from the sea, opposed by the lofty wall of precipice, rushed upwards, and bursting over the margin above with a force much increased by compression, in fierce gusts, often brought the travellers to a dead stand for several minutes together. The terrific howlings of the wind, as it rushed up those steeps, and the roar of the waters breaking in fury against the rocks below, together with the proximity of the pathway to the awful abysses, made the journey of our travellers, on that tempestuous night, as exciting and perilous, so far as we know, as any in the records of wild adventure. It was indeed a dreadful night, says the story, but it had no terrors for the aged priest, who sat through all in quiet unconcern on his brave little steed.

About half-way between Malinbeg and the One Man's Path, the footway touched the very verge of a beetling cliff, from which a good view of portions of the steeps farther on is obtained. When the tra-

vellers neared the edge of the precipice, the wind
unexpectedly ceased. " Owen, my son," said the
old man, " this sudden calm bodes no good. I should
not be surprised if we had a whirlwind up the precipices directly." Owen shuddered, brave though he
was. " True, Father, true for you : better let us go
back from the edge and lie down for a little." " No
need of hurry, Owen ; the gray pony is sure. Just
let us look over, and see if anything is going on below." The moon was shining brightly at the moment.
They moved to the extreme edge of the precipice.
The priest pointing with his riding cane, spoke in a
somewhat excited tone : " Look ! look ! the whirl-
wind is under the One Man's Path. See that dark
spot ! It is lifting the water." The phenomenon
was not new to the veteran priest, neither was the
clerk entirely unacquainted with it. It was one of
those tornadoes that form at the base of those sea-
cliffs. The clerk felt real alarm. " Let us go back !"
he exclaimed—" back at once ! it may come this
way, and if it do, woe betide us." " Don't be afraid,
Owen," said the priest, " I have seen the like of this
before now. It seems as if all the wind from Traban to Carrigan Head was gathered into that little
spot, whirling round and round, one part driving
the other before it faster and faster every instant.
Halloa ! it comes round this way ; it did wild work,

I'm sure, on the other side of that precipice. See, it stops !—it is held for a moment between the rocks. Oh ! how it eddies on the surface of the water, trying to screw its way down through it ; but it cannot, and therefore it lashes the water against the precipices. Ha ! now it rises. We must be alive, Owen, it may come upon us. See, there it goes up the steeps with the strength of ten thousand giants !" The effects of the phenomenon, as it ascended in a slanting direction, were almost too terrible to be grand. Rising at first like a dense cloud, it lifted a quantity of the water, which it dashed into thin spray on the rocks, and sent it here and there in shoots, or water-spouts, far up the steeps, leaving the sea below in a fury frightful to behold. On it came up the precipices, toppling crags of stone and heaps of gravel, displacing rocks, tearing out pieces of earth, sweeping plots of shingle, and sending the debris tumbling down in promiscuous confusion, accompanied by a deep rumbling noise, as if the whole mountain was going to pieces. The travellers withdrew quickly into the moor, keeping the while an eye on the course of the tornado. The clerk was sore afraid, and the priest himself now began to be anxious, for the tornado was coming towards them. He dismounted, and holding the bridle firmly in his hand, led the pony back still farther into the moor. "Owen, can you find no place where we might lie down and hold by. That tornado is so strong that it will lift us off the earth like straws." Owen could find nothing else to hold by than the scanty grass of the moor. "It will never do," said the priest. The terrible whirlwind approached them steadily. They were crouching in its direct course. A pause, and the priest exclaimed, "We are safe, thank God!" By one of those eccentric movements usual to those eddying winds, it stopped short, and taking a nearly contrary direction, it mounted up the steep side of Slieve League's loftiest peak, and spent itself among the heights. "Owen," said the priest, as he rose from the ground and remounted his pony, "do not the angels guard us? The storm is over; that is the last kick of the dying giant."

Nothing daunted, but, on the contrary, considerably animated by the terrible incidents of the last quarter of an hour, and a certain religious enthusiasm, they went forward on their difficult path, up a very steep ascent, culminating in the highest point of the mountain, and immediately struck upon the One Man's Path. It were hard to imagine a more perilous road for a horseman than this narrow edge between yawning abysses. The priest without hesitation rode his sure-footed pony out on the dizzy

footway, the clerk following behind.   Presently
the pony came to a dead stand, and turning its head
over the awful precipice began to snort.   The priest
patted it on the neck to quiet it.   " Owen, did you
hear any strange sound ? " " The Lord preserve us ! "
was Owen's only reply.   Both listened with breath-
less attention.   A long deep groan, as of a man
suffering intense pain, came floating up from below
in the now calm air ; and, after a brief interval,
another, and then another.   The priest dismounted,
or rather slid from his horse.   " Owen, that is some
poor Christian in sore distress, perhaps both of soul
and body.   There is a wreck below,—I can see the
spars breaking the surface of the swells.   Stay you
here with the pony, and don't attempt to move till
I return."   " For God's sake, Father, take care.   Do
you mean to throw yourself down the precipices ? "
" Don't be alarmed, my son ; when I was young I
often traversed these steeps, for though they over-
hang the sea, they have hollows and rents.   God
often takes good out of evil ; I know every crevice
and step down here, and what I did then for vanity,
will enable me now, perhaps, to save a poor soul.
True, it needs great strength of muscle as well as of
nerve to scramble down this wild place, but though
I'm old my feet are still used to the rocks, and I feel
myself as strong this blessed night as I was forty

years ago." The old man spoke thus, while he divested himself of his muffler and great-coat, and having consigned them to the clerk, he let himself out over the verge of the cliff, and descended, using feet and hands with marvellous dexterity, repeating as he disappeared, " And better than all, Owen, the angels guard us."

"The angels guard him!" echoed the clerk, almost unconscious of what he was saying. After four long hours of awful suspense on his airy watch-tower, the course of his musings was suddenly interrupted by a sudden change in the demeanour of the horse, which sagacious animal began all at once to neigh, and paw the ground, and to start, as if gathering itself for a spring over the precipice. The next thing that attracted him was the priest's voice, and the priest himself presently came scrambling up and stood before him. He reached the clerk his hand, " Owen, my son, do not the angels guard us ?" The clerk seized the proffered hand in both his, and kissed it with passionate reverence ; but it was strange that so voluble and so curious a man as Owen was known to be did not utter a word, nor did he ask a single question till they had crossed the One Man's Path and got down into the valley of Teelin. Then his tongue was loosened, and he had many a question to ask, and the priest gratified him with a full account of his adventure down the cliff.

Father Carr, directed by the groans which issued at regular intervals from a recess in the precipice below, reached the spot, and found a man in a dying condition lying there. He was a Spaniard, and, as the priest had studied in Spain, a communication was easily opened between them. The history of the stranger contained a deep lesson. He had been blessed with a good and pious mother, whom he loved dearly, who, when he was a little child, taught him, among many pious prayers, a short petition for the assistance of a priest at his death, and she used to make him promise to say this prayer every night before going to bed. She fell ill and died while he was yet a boy. He grew up into a dissipated young man, but through all his excesses he continued to repeat the short prayer taught him by his mother, whose memory he ever cherished with deep affection. After dissipating his fortune at home, he emigrated to the Spanish settlements in the West Indies. Here he changed his ways. Turning all the resources of his mind to the pursuit of gain, he soon grew rich, and after the lapse of many years, an eager longing for home possessed him. He turned what he could of his property into cash, and set sail for Spain with all his wealth, in the safest ship that frequented the West Indian waters. A strong southerly wind, blowing the whole time of the voyage, bore the vessel to the north far out of her course, so that when she reached this side of the Atlantic she was standing into Donegal Bay. She was caught in the tempest of that evening, and as the early part of the night was dark, the captain did not observe accurately his proximity to the shore. When the moon rose, revealing, by its fitful gleams, the precipitous cliffs of Slieve League, the crew did all they could to keep the vessel off the rocks, but the wind growing stronger every moment, proved too many for them.

When all hope was given over, the Spaniard took a sum of gold coin, and putting it into a leathern girdle used by him in long and dangerous journeys as a purse, fastened it tightly round his waist. He had hardly come up on deck, when the ship, now close to the rocks, was spun round by a whirl-wind, soon to be broken and left floating in small splinters among the breakers. The familiar prayer taught him by his long-lost mother came to the lips of the Spaniard, and he repeated it fervently as he sank into the mighty waters. After his immersion he rose to the surface, and being an expert swimmer, he struck boldly for the shore, when the seething waters through which he was cutting his way suddenly rushed back with great force, dragging him over pointed rocks. He now felt a sense of blindness and suffocation from the foam, and his head seemed to him to be bending, as if from the repeated buffets of waves, till it was turned completely under, and then he seemed to himself to be sinking, sinking, sinking, head downwards, into awful depths. He lost all consciousness from that moment, till, awaking from a dream in which he saw the sweet face of his mother, and felt the gentle pressure of her hand while she bathed his throbbing temples with a sponge, he found himself stretched face downwards on a ledge of rock barely out of the reach of the waves which at frequent intervals sent a shower of spray on the cliffs above him. He was not long in realising the danger of his position, and, though sadly wounded by the tossing among the sharp rocks, he began to crawl upwards, resting every now and then, till at length he lay down exhausted in the recess in which Father Carr had found him. While he lay there he repeated many a prayer with deep earnestness, but none more fervently than the one he cherished so dearly for his mother's sake, and at each repetition of it he groaned bitterly at the reflection that he made himself unworthy of its being heard. Those were the groans that drew the priest to the spot.

The feelings of the Spaniard may be more easily imagined than described when he found that a priest, speaking his mother's tongue, knelt beside him. His strength was failing fast ; the cold chill of death was creeping over his members. He had just time to tell his history to the good priest, to whom he handed over the gold he had upon his person to build a chapel in thanksgiving for this great grace. The priest having shrived him and administered to him all the consolations of his religion, the Spaniard died, and his remains were afterwards laid in a decent resting-place. The chapel was built in due time, and the passer-by may still see the remains of it on the road-side between Kilcar and Carrick ;—it is called the " Chapel of the Spaniard" to this day.

II. Excursion to Glencolumbkille.

" A visit should by all means be paid to Glen, a district which tourists should not fail to explore, instead of stopping short at Slieve League, as most are content to do."* For the first two miles the road ascends along the Owenwee river, having Slieve League on the right. There is a cross-road *left* at Lough-oona, the road to the left descending into

* Murray.

the Glen of Malinmore, and that to the right leading into Glencolumbkille—the glen of the celebrated
St Colum Cille, and the Sean-Glean, of which mention is often made in Irish ecclesiastical history.
The road passing Loughunshagh falls rapidly into
the valley.   Far down the Glen are a Catholic
chapel close to the road, and a Protestant church
farther to the right, which stands on the site probably occupied by the old monastery of St Columba.
At a turn in the road there is a stone cross, which
there is every reason to believe, from the evidence
of the monument itself, as well from the traditions
of the place, was placed there by the saint himself.
A little farther down, on a slope on the northern
side, is the saint's well, and adjoining it is the saint's
bed, where probably there was a cell, to which the
saint withdrew from time to time, at a short distance from the monastery.

   Glen is seen to best advantage in the pensive
hour of evening.   It opens on the sea, the valley
terminating in a strand, on which the waves of the
Atlantic break for ever.   The hill that encloses it
on the northern side presents a fine escarpment,
breaking into precipices, where it runs out and forms
the noble ocean cliff called Glen Head.   It is in
very truth a retreat to the mind of the pious con-
templative, who, in this remote vale, shut in be-

tween Slieve League and Slieveatooey, may have his meditations on the divine attributes quickened and elevated into higher contemplations, by the presence of some of the sublimest and most awful aspects of nature.

III. Excursion Round Glen Head and Slieveatooey to Ardara.

The cliff scenery round Glen Head and Slieveatooey is only second to that of Slieve League. The tourist therefore should not fail to explore it. It will hardly take away from its charm that but the fewest of the very few who visit the coast scenery of Donegal make this excursion. Our tourist, then, may set out with the idea that he is "doing" the next thing to crossing some lofty, unexplored alp. He will need to start early, as he will have to traverse a coast line of some eighteen miles from Glen to Ardara. If he make the hotel at Carrick his starting-point, he should take a car to Glen, which he might order to meet him on the other side of Slieveatooey, on the Maghery road, or at the police barrack at the head of Glengesh, to take him to see that fine glen, and thence to Ardara.

But the tourist may spend the night before this excursion at Miss Walker's of Malinmore, a nearer starting-point by four miles than Carrick. The road round to Glen (2 miles) is capital, and affords exciting views of Glen Bay. It will be easy to find a guide in Glen; the first intelligent peasant you meet will do. There is a bridle path some two miles over the headland. The tourist will easily identify Glen Head by the martello tower which stands here within a short distance of the verge of the cliff. Having surveyed this cliff, which rises eight hundred feet from the water, he should ask his guide to lead on to the Sturrell, or *Camas-binne*, (Bent-cliff,) keeping close to the margin all the way, in order to enjoy the views of the precipices from different points along the line of this serrated coast. In general, these headlong steeps present an even front, awful for their unbroken altitude, the predominating colour being a pale yellow, with lines of watercourses and landslips here and there running from the top to the bottom. In the crevices of the rocks there are sparse scraps of grasses, which, awful as are the precipices, the natives sometimes come at by being swung down from above.

A gravelled path leads to a seat on the brow of the sheer precipice, from which the visitor may, without a sense of insecurity, survey the *Sturrell.* This most extraordinary cliff juts out from the line of precipices that here form the coast. It is almost insulated, being connected with the main range by a narrow neck rising up steeply on both sides, and terminating in a sharp edge at the top. Beyond this edge the peninsula widens somewhat, and attains to the height of 850 feet. There are some patches of bright herbage which relieve pleasantly the weather-beaten face of the precipices. The visitor should take care not to trust himself among these steeps, which on the northern side do not appear from a distance so impracticable as they really are. A few of the natives, whose legs and heads have been formed to the cliffs by long habit, venture all round this enormous breakwater in quest of birds' nests, or the sweet grasses that grow in the crevices.

The tourist should now proceed to the *Sawpit*, which is a cleft of about seven feet in width, hewn right through one of the precipices. The visitor can pass down through this open, picking his steps over loose stones, to within about fifty feet of the waves. The especial characteristics of the *Sawpit* are the precipices which rise on either side of the narrow passage like walls of finely chiselled stone, joined with exquisite art, and vertical as a plumb-line. The wall on the left, as you look down the cleft, advances into the sea considerably beyond that on

I

the right. Below the point where the latter breaks off, the rock sinks into an even slope falling gently to the waves. The visitor might be tempted to step on this rocky embankment, but if he do, he has need of great caution, for a slip might lead to destruction, as the surface presents few inequalities for either hand or foot to hold by.

About a mile further on there is a break in the coast line, and a strip of strand, forming a little harbour called Purt, or Port, a name which can properly be applied to it only by comparison with the other portions of this inhospitable coast. At the northern extremity of this indentation the precipices appear again in great magnificence, and *Tormore*, the centre of a group of insulated boulders, begins now to be a conspicuous object. Inland, there is a valley in the bleak moor, a few green fields, and a group of four cottages of the humblest kind, built without reference to aspect or road—for here road there is none. Crossing a brawling brook, the russet bed of which may betoken mineral wealth in the bowels of the mountains, but does not tempt the passing traveller to linger by its waters, the tourist ascends Port Hill, bidding his guide lead to the cliff adjacent to the *Tormore*. Cautiously surveying his ground as he advances, he should approach the edge of the precipice, which sinks sheer down, sharp and clean as a knife. Here, on this vantage ground, raised 818 feet above the level of the ocean, he may rest awhile to contemplate the scene before him.

The geologist will strive to determine, according to the conditions of his theory, whether the family of rocks scattered here amidst the waves of the Atlantic are the fragments of a mountain torn by the war of elements, or have risen from the ocean, destined to serve as the foundation on which a new mountain shall in time be built. An instructive lesson, surely, and of a noble science, may thus be gained. But a yet nobler lesson is suggested by the scene. The mountain solitudes, the awful cliffs round whose base the waves rage and roar for ever, the vast limitless ocean stretching far into the horizon, and beyond it the sky stretching farther still, until it is lost in the unimaginable depths of space,— all kindle in the soul the feeling of the infinite ; and the little thing man is, is, in the comparison, annihilated by the sense of the majesty and the power whose presence is here recognized. Salutary lesson of greatness and of nothingness ! The man must have an ill constituted mind, who can stand here to contemplate the scene around him, and not feel his soul glow with emotion. The least thoughtful will think of Him who " compassed the sea with its bounds, and set a law to the waters that they should not pass their limits."

An incident related to the writer, in view of the spot, lends a melancholy interest to the *Tormore.* One morning, not many years ago, a boy, who had been in the habit of visiting this cliff from time to time in quest of the nests of the birds of this wild region, came here to ply his dangerous trade. In very calm weather, one well acquainted with the intricacies of the coast can make his way at low water from this island-rock to the mainland. This day, however, a storm rose suddenly, which the boy, engaged in his exciting occupation, did not perceive in time, so when he came to cross to the shore he found himself encircled by breakers. The storm lasted for more than a week, and during the whole of that time the waves continued to beat round the rock with unabated fury, rendering all approach to it, or departure from it, certain destruction. The boy died of cold and hunger on that desolate crag, which, however, furnished clay enough to cover his remains, and he was buried on a narrow ledge high up the precipitous side of the rock.

Peaceful be thy slumbers, poor boy! Thy trade was a dangerous one, and thou hast paid for thy hardihood a dear reckoning. The winds and the waves, making common cause with the sea fowl, conspired to crush thee, and thou wast in truth a feeble reed in the midst of their warring circle. Still thou hadst that in thee which made thee greater than they; thou hadst *knowledge* of thy end, they were unconscious of their power. Thou wast immeasurably less than they in the part of thee that was of earth, but infinitely greater in the part of thee that is immortal. Even now thou hast thy triumph. The awful accompaniments that made thy death so terrible still surround thy tomb. The waves and the winds make ceaseless moan around thee, and the screams of the wild sea-bird mingle with the sad dirge that goes on for ever. And for thy resting place thou hast found a monument greater than column or pyramid ever raised to hold the bones of earthly potentate.

If the visitor be a poet, the history of this poor boy is a fit theme for an effort. The rock itself is already admirably characterized in Keats's noble address—

> " Hearken, thou craggy ocean pyramid!
>   Give answer from thy voice, the sea-fowl's screams!
>   When were thy shoulders mantled in huge streams ?
> When, from the sun, was thy broad forehead hid ?
> How long is 't since thy mighty power bid
>   Thee heave to airy sleep from fathom dreams ?
>   Sleep in the lap of thunder or sun-beams,
> Or when gray clouds are thy cover-lid ?
> Thou answer'st not, for thou art dead asleep !

Thy life is but two dead eternities—
The last in air, the former in the deep ;
 First with the whales, last with the eagle-skies—
Drown'd wast thou till one earthquake made thee steep,
 Another cannot wake thy giant size."

A curious story is told, and universally believed in Glen, to the effect that it had been for some time the last hiding place of the Pretender, ere he was able to make his way from the shores of these kingdoms. The Rev. Mr Griffiths, the late incumbent of Glencolumbkille, has ably discussed this tradition in a paper published some years since in the *Dublin University Magazine,* which they who take an interest in the details of English history should read. It would be worth the historian's while to examine the grounds of this interesting belief. According to the tradition, the Prince used to spend the greater part of the day stretched on this headland, looking out for the ship which was to convey him to another country.

The tourist should continue his route close to the coast, which retains its precipitous character throughout ; and, as it is serrated, he will gain various and exciting views of these marvellous steeps along his path to *Puliska,* where an indentation forms a basin of calm water amidst surroundings the most savage it is possible to conceive. Looking out from any of those airy headlands on the vast expanse of ocean, one gets the idea of its immensity, its beauty of line and colour and others of its attributes. Still, from your high position the sea below seems calm, the swells look shadows passing over the waters, and the surges like the breaking of the ripples on a quiet lake. But if you could get into a boat, and move a stone's throw from the shore, the water completely loses this gentle character.

Among the most profound and the most vividly remembered emotions produced in the mind of the writer by anything he has seen in nature, were those he received while passing under the cliffs of Slieveatooey, at the entrance into Puliska. The starting point was Dowros, some eight miles to the northeast. The weather had been beautiful for weeks before, and that morning was so fine that there was hardly wind enough to fill our sail. The sea was, as the phrase goes, at rest. Once fairly out in the deep, the element that had appeared to us from the shore to lie in calm and peaceful slumber, gave no token of a fixed law or a regular succession of incidents. Now it is nothing but a broken surface of wave-crests in wild disorder. Sitting here on a level equal with the waves themselves, you realize the restlessness, the fitful change, the unfathomable depth, the irresistible might, the unsubdued power of the ocean. Our little boat moves lazily across the sound, and passes into the shadow of Slieveatooey. As we advance, rocks that were before unseen now appear ahead above the surface, and other rocks that were visible only as specks in the distance rise up like sable monsters from the deep, and a thin margin of beautiful white turned out to be an array of surges that we dared not approach. Advancing still, we come closer to the shore. Threatening us on our left rose the cliffs of Slieveatooey, darkening half of the heavens; close ahead of us a precipice projected a short way into the sea, and the waves broke upon it with great fury; while just opposite, at a short distance, was an island rock of a large size, rising not more than two or three feet above the sea-level;—on this the swell rose tremulous, and broke just at the instant it was leaving it, making the place a circle of foam, in the midst of which the black area of the rock immediately began to appear above the water, as the spray danced in a thousand miniature fountains down its edge. The narrow passage between this rock and the precipice opposite was white with foam. The two breakers seemed to meet, so narrow was the space between them. Beyond this white line was literally a forest of islanded rocks, round which the waters surged in unappeasable anger, and fretted in the open spaces. It seemed as if we were borne by some irresistible destiny into a region of horrors.

The boatmen saw alarm in some of our faces. "No fear, no fear," they said, as they brought our frail skiff slowly between the two watery walls that threatened to engulph us. It was not till after we had got clear of our Scylla and Charybdis that there was real need of caution. Suddenly one of our boatmen dashed his oar into the water, and with two or three powerful strokes turned the bow of the boat towards the rocks, and then both pulling together in strong, rapid strokes, the little vessel bounded forward on the crest of a great wave, and in a moment we were gliding silently through the calm water of Puliska. Here we found ourselves within a circle of rough naked rocks, standing round in grim array, like so many giants ready to smite any one who should dare to invade those solitudes. Within, a cascade of considerable volume tumbled down a deep ravine, cut through the precipice, sheer into the water of the basin. Towards this point our boat glided, and stopped near it, alongside a narrow ledge of rock. One of the boatmen stepped out, and led the way, the rest of the party climbing up the steep precipice after him.

If the tourist's visit to this part of the coast fall on particularly fine weather, he should by all means explore this region from the sea. He can learn at Ardara where he is most likely to find a boat. The most convenient starting place is Loughros Point, some two or three miles from Ardara ; but a good arrangement would be, to walk the headland to Puliska, and have a boat waiting at that place, which is the centre of the most interesting part of the scenery. There are many marine caves under Slieveatooey, which the boatmen of the neighbourhood speak of with great enthusiasm. The writer feels bound to say, that he has not seen these caves, though he has often tried to do so. The approach to them is so guarded by dangerous breakers, that it is rarely one can effect an entrance. He has heard, however, from intelligent gentlemen, whose attempts were more fortunate than his own, that these marine chambers almost surpass imagination, presenting a perfect labyrinth of subterranean architecture.

The precipitous side of Slieveatooey rising over Puliska is precarious, and the tourist, therefore, had better follow up, for a short distance, the course of the Glenlough river, which here brings its brief career to so striking an end, and then face up the mountain. He will not fail to notice that the virgin solitude is broken by a solitary tenement, the lone habitation of one Burke, a shepherd,

> " Whose precious charge,
> Nibble their fill at ocean's very marge." *

---

* Keats's *Endymion.*

The tourist should now ascend Glenlough Hill, from the summit of which a view singularly fine opens out before him. To the north-east, the deeply indented coast presents a rapid succession of creek and headland, receding in glorious perspective all the way to the distant Bloody Foreland. The visitor should here consult his map, as he is in a capital position from which to get a clear notion of the part of Donegal that faces the Atlantic. Below him is Loughrosbeg Bay, running up in a narrow creek under the mountain on which he stands, (called Slieveatooey, that is, "Mountain to the North," because it is the northern side of the peninsula whose coast he has been exploring since he left Killybegs.) Beyond is Loughros Point, a flat tongue of land dotted with neat-looking cottages, and then Loughrosmore Bay, with its extensive tideway stretching up to Ardara, a "lurking town," (to use Wordsworth's beautiful expression,) from which you may trace the valley of the Owenea as far as Glenties, where it enters a beautiful glen running some five miles into the heart of the mountains. Behind Glenties rises the noble Aghla, whose northern base is washed by Lough Finn. On the northern side of Loughrosmore Bay is Kiltouris Lough, on an island of which was a castle belonging to the O'Boyles, the ruling sept in this district, which still retains their name.

Dowros Head and Crohy Head are two bold promontories guarding Boylagh, or Gweebarra Bay, at the head of which is a long, narrow estuary, running inland till it is lost from your view between steeply escarped hills. Beyond Crohy Head is a coast marvellously irregular, from its many indentations and the multitude of islands that cover the blue waters in that region; high above all which is Arranmore, standing out in the sea, as if to protect the others from the violence of the Atlantic. Rutland, looking like an enormous sandbank, and Owey, in the distance, are also conspicuous objects in the panorama.

The scenery of Slieveatooey itself is of absorbing interest. The whole northern face of the mountain is precipitously steep, and will keep the visitor, who scrambles—which ought to be done with great caution—above its precipices, constantly excited. These inaccessible steeps, like those of Slieve League, are still the favourite haunt of the eagle, so that there is a chance of meeting a member of the royal species in these remote regions; and here, if anywhere, may the royal bird revel in unrestrained freedom; for rarely, indeed, does the voice of human being break those solitudes.

> "And sure there is a secret power that reigns
> Here, where no trace of man the spot profanes,
> Nought but the herds, that, pasturing upward, creep,
> Hung dim-discovered from the dangerous steep."*

---

* Wordsworth.

The highest point of the mountain is Croagh Ballagh-down, standing 1692 feet over the sea, its altitude seeming much greater than it really is, on account of the steep escarpment down to the water. The tourist may now keep along the ridge of the mountain to join the main route at Glengesh barrack, and descend by the Glengesh pass into Ardara, or he may take the headlong path that drops into the wild Granny Glen to Maghery, where a few cottages are nestling under the shadow of the mountain. In the immediate neighbourhood are half-a-dozen caves, three of which run in narrow passages, like corridors in a catacomb, some hundreds of yards right into the bowels of the mountain. The most interesting of these "Coves," as they are here called, is the Cooach-an-Darchadass, (the Dark-cave,) which may be entered only at low-water. The visitor may easily find a guide among the Maghery people, and he should not forget to provide a torch or candle, without which much of the interest of his visit would be lost. From Maghery to Ardara, his path lies at the base of the mountain, down whose steep side leaps many a brawling mountain torrent. There is a splendid waterfall, called Asherancally, about half-a-mile from Maghery, which deserves a special visit, should the tourist happen to be in this neighbourhood during rainy weather. His road is now along the base of the mountain to Brackey, where he joins the main route, at a short distance from Ardara. It is now evening and he may fairly note down—

> " Many the wonders I this day have seen ;
> The sun when first he kist away the tears
> That filled the eyes of morn :
> The ocean with its vastness, its blue green,
> Its ships, its rocks, its caves, its hopes, its fears,—
> Its voice mysterious, which whoso hears
> Must think of what will be, and what has been."*

CARRICK TO ARDARA.

The tourist who proceeds by the direct route from Carrick to Ardara, takes the road that runs parallel with the Glen river for some distance, and then leaves it to follow up the course of the Crove river. After a long stretch of bleak Highland moor, relieved, however, by some bold elevations on the right, and glimpses of the sea, with the island of Aranmore in the distance, on the left, the watershed (1000 feet) is reached, when all at once he finds himself right above the most striking glen, perhaps, he has anywhere seen. A spiral road brings him down the quick descent into the valley of Glengesh, or Glengeask, having Croaghalery on the left, rising some 1200 feet steeply from the road, and on the right Glengesh hill, standing 1652 feet over the sea level.

* Keats.—To his brother George.

At about two miles down the Glen the road emerges from these mountain walls, and, a little farther on, joining the road from Killybegs, turns sharply and pursues its way through a pretty valley overlooked by steep hills to

ARDARA, "which has an extremely pretty situation at the wooded base of steeply escarped hills." * It is a good centre from whence to explore the magnificent coast scenery of Slieveatooey. It is also a good centre for the lover of sport—there being good grouse-shooting and good fishing in the neighbourhood. Close to the town are a shooting lodge, at present rented by the Earl of Gosford, and Woodhill, a neglected residence belonging to the Rev. Mr Tredenick. There is also a Danish fort above the northern extremity of the town. From Ardara the road follows up the valley of the Owentucker river, an interesting drive affording a rich variety of Highland views. Towards the end of the third mile, from a high point of the road, there is a striking view of Glenties and its background of mountains ; a view which has been finely expressed by Mr Falkner in a painting exhibited by him in the Dublin Exhibition of 1864. At the end of the fourth mile, the road approaches the bank of the Owenea, a river that derives its name and source

* Murray.

from Lough Ea, a tarn some six miles away among the mountains, and crossing the stream a little higher up passes into

GLENTIES, "a small town, the situation of which, at the numerous converging glens, is its best point. It has a grand-looking Union-house, which adds much to the distant beauty of the place," [*] as does also the Catholic chapel—a spacious building occupying a commanding position above the town. Glenties is one of the four towns in the county of Donegal, in which Quarter Sessions are held, and is also a central police station. It is the centre of the barony of Boylagh, of which Lewis remarked thirty years ago, that it was remarkable for its "woollen stockings of excellent quality." [†] This department of Irish manufacture, which had wofully declined during the past five-and-twenty years, has lately received a fresh impulse. The tourist who takes an interest in the manufactural produce of the country, should pay a visit to the well-appointed warehouse of the firm of D. & H. MacDevitt, where he will see various specimens—some of them very beautiful— of the hand-knit hose produced in the district. Excellent grouse shooting is to be had in the neighbourhood, and good fishing also on the river and lakes. "The angler in the river (Owenea) will have

---

[*] Murray.   [†] Topograph. Dict. Art. Donegal.

sport, if he is on at the time of a spate, but as it rises and falls very quickly, it will be hardly worth his while to go there on a chance."* The Marquis of Conyngham is the owner of Glenties, and is spoken of in fair terms in the neighbourhood. The antiquary will find, in a field adjoining the road, close to the town, one of those pillar-stones, "which evidently owe their upright position, not to accident, but to the design and labour of an ancient people."† This specimen is more slender and graceful than most examples of pillar-stone, though it stands only six feet over the surface of the ground. About half-a-mile from the town, crowning a hill, called from the circumstance the *Castle,* are the remains of what, it is almost certain, was one of those stone *Cathairs* or *Duns,* belonging to the Pagan period, the ruins of which are found so common along the southern and western coasts of Ireland. The visitor ought to note the fact, that the thick wall enclosing the very extensive farm, at the head of which the "Castle" stood, is built of stones taken from the fort in the memory of people still living. Enough remains to enable him to trace the circular wall enclosing about an acre of the crest of the hill ; the rest he must supply from what he knows of works

---

* Murray.   † Wakeman's Handbook of Irish Antiquities.

of its class—from examples elsewhere remaining in a more perfect state of preservation.*

Distances.—Ardara, 6 miles; Narin, 8½; Ducarry, 10; Dungloe, 18; Fintown, 7; Killybegs, 14; Donegal, 18; Stranorlar, 21; Letterkenny, 23.

I.—Excursion to Narin.

The greater portion of the first two miles is over a bleak moor, but from every point of the road fine mountain views are obtained. At the third mile a detour should be made by the road leading to the right, to Portachurry, to join the direct route again at Maas, which road, carried along the steep declivities of the Derryloughan hills, abounds in exciting incident, and affords beautiful views of the Gweebarra Bay. The tourist will be struck with the marvellous profusion in which granite boulders —some of them gigantic blocks—are sown broadcast on the surface of the ground over which he is passing.

"Narin is a primitive little fishing village, plea-

* Staigue Fort, in the county of Kerry, is one of the most perfect *Cathairs* remaining in Ireland. "It consists of a circular wall of uncemented stones, about eighteen feet in height, and twelve in thickness, enclosing an area of eighty-eight yards in diameter. Upon the internal face of the wall are regular flights of steps, leading to the highest part of the building. The doorway is composed of large unhewn stones, and is covered by a horizontal lintel." —Wakeman's Handbook of Irish Antiquities, p. 46.

santly situated opposite the island of Inniskeel, on
which the antiquary will find a couple of ruined
churches."*   A monastery was founded in this
island, at a very remote period, by St Connell, who
is mentioned in the Martyrology of Donegal, under
May 22d, as follows :—" Connall, Abbot of Inis-
Caoil, in Cinel Connaill, and he is himself of Cinel
Connaill." The saint's paternal name was *Caoil*,
and hence the name Inis-Caoil, pronounced Inis-
keel. It is a great resort for pilgrims, who come
here in large numbers during the summer months
to beg the intercession of St Connell. Inniskeel
gives its name to the parish, the most extensive one
by the way, as far as acres go, in the county. The
glebe-house (Rev. J. Ovens,) is hidden under the
rocky head of Castlegoland hill, but the little church
occupies a commanding position over the sea. Opposite the island, to the south, is a coast-guard
station, at Portnoo. "This whole promontory, between Narin and Ardara, is worth exploring for the
sake of the remains. On Dunmore hill, a headland
one mile to the west, there are ten old forts. It
was probably the grand signal-station, so that a
signal made there would alarm the rest." † The
view from this hill is fine, embracing the magnificent cliffs of Slieveatooey, and the mountains above

* Murray.   † Ibid.

Glenties, forming a splendid range with the more distant peaks of the Glendowan, Slieve-Snaght, and Errigle. On the other side of the Gweebarra Bay is the bold headland of Crohy, whilst out towards the north the island of Arranmore forms a striking feature.

In the moor above Narin is Lough Doon, on which there is a Bawan in a tolerable state of preservation. Its circular wall encloses the whole area of a small island near the shore. Not far from Lough Doon is Lough Birroge, on which there is a similar remain, and about a mile further on is Kiltooris Lough, at the east side of which is Eden House, (G. Hamilton, Esq.,) and at the west side, on an island close to the shore, are the remains of a castle belonging to the O'Boyles, once the lords and masters of Boylagh.

From this place a hilly road leads to Kilclooney, where there is a *Cromlech,* near the road, at a short distance beyond the Catholic chapel. The table, or covering stone, measures about eighteen feet from east to west, about twenty from north to south, and from six to eight in thickness. This gigantic slab slopes with a considerable incline towards the west. Close to this larger "bed," as it is called, is another of about one-third its dimensions. Both are enclosed by a stone circle. As the people of the locality never call this monument by the name of *Cromlech*, the visitor should ask to have *Lebacha Diarmid agus Grainné*, or the beds of *Diarmid* and *Grainné*, pointed out to him, a designation which has originated in a very ancient and popular tale. The famous Cormac Mac Art had a daughter, Grainné, celebrated far and wide for her personal charms, whom the still more famous Finn Mac Cumhal solicited in marriage. Cormac was favourable to the hero's suit, and, accordingly, to his court at Tara came Finn, attended by a chosen body of warriors, amongst whom were his son Oisin, his grandson Oscar, and Diarmid O'Duibhnè, one of his chief officers. A banquet, suitable to the occasion and the dignity of the guests, was prepared, at which the beautiful Grainné did the honours of mistress of the mansion. It was the custom in those remote times for the lady presiding at table to fill a rich drinking-cup with the choicest liquor, and to send it round to be tasted by the guests. In due time Grainné's precious cup was carried round by her maid until all drank of it except Oisin and Diarmid, and as the bowl passed, great was the praise pronounced by all on the delicious draught. But the murmur of compliment quickly subsided into deathlike silence, for the liquor in which they pledged the young hostess proved a powerful narcotic that threw every one that had tasted it into a profound sleep. Having thus far succeeded, she appealed to the characteristic chivalry of Oisin and Diarmid to rescue her from an overwhelming misery. Finn was an old and war-worn man. How could she consent to become his wife? But as her father had agreed to the match, the only way to escape the deep misfortune was by flight. Oisin, of course, could not dishonour his own father, but Diarmid could become her partner and protector. The lady's eloquence prevailed. Diarmid and Grainné bade a hasty adieu to Oisin and departed. Great was the rage of King Cormac and Finn, when they awoke from their trance, to find that the bird had flown. The renowned Finn started at once in pursuit, and the sequel occupies the chief portion of an interesting Fenian romance. *

Looking to the east, from Kilclooney, the visitor will easily identify Carnaween, the highest point in the mountain range in that quarter. On this lofty summit there is another *Cromlech*, and, according to the legend told in the mountains, the fugitives succeeded thus for a time in eluding pursuit. Finn, as all the world knows, had a tooth of divination, which he consulted in all his difficulties by putting

* "The Pursuit of Diarmid and Grainné," with a literal translation, has been published a few years since by the Ossianic Society.

his thumb under it. When Diarmid had passed the first night at Kilclooney, being prevented by the sea from going farther, he took with him a sack of sand and returned by a detour to Carnaween, where he spread the sand on his bed. Meanwhile, Finn applied his thumb to the divination tooth, and received for answer that the pair were passing the night on the sand. He went, accordingly, to the bed at Kilclooney, and was of course disappointed. Next morning, Diarmid having concealed his bag of sand, took a bundle of heath, returned to, and spent the night in the bed at Kilclooney. Finn, as usual, when the night came consulted his tooth, and got for answer that the pair were passing the night on the heath, and he accordingly sought the pair at Carnaween. Thus was the giant baffled, his gift of divination notwithstanding. From Kilclooney the tourist may proceed to Ardara, or return to Glenties by Loughfad.

II.—EXCURSION THROUGH THE GLENS.

The lover of Highland scenery may have a pleasant excursion of some ten miles, through two glens that are hidden in the mountains behind Glenties. About a mile and a half from Glenties, a sadly neglected road is given off the main road to the right, and passing under Aughla mountain, ascends

Stracastle Glen, which, at the lower end is strikingly wild, but softens as you ascend farther into the mountains. At about four miles the road crosses the Stracastle river, the passage over this Highland stream consisting of a few large stones, laid at regular intervals, edgeways, under the water, and is carried over a tract of hilly upland for about two miles, when it drops into the Glenmore, and holds an even tenor along the Owenea to Glenties. The reader will find some details of this beautiful Glenmore in the excursion from Stranorlar to Glenties.

III.—Excursion to Dungloe.

Leaving Glenties, the main route is followed up to the third mile, where the direct road to Dungloe goes off to the left up Derryloghan hill, and then turning to the right, keeps along the southern shore of the Gweebarra estuary for seven miles to Ducarry.

The shore facing the north is bleak, rocky, and untenanted, but the opposite shore, a district called Lettermacaward, is cultivated, and thickly dotted with cottages. The estuary lies at your feet all the way, and there is a view of the valley running inland as far as the mountains of Slieve Snaght and Glendowan. From the more elevated part of the ground good distant views to the north-east are obtained. From Ducarry, you ascend by a zig-zag road, the steep side on the north of the Gweebarra, and looking back, you get a striking view of the pass running up to Lough-Barra, and the distant mountain ranges. When you have fairly attained the high ground, your "way lies through an un-tameably wild country, but with such shifting panoramas of mountains, that the attention is never fatigued."* Away to the right are the Glendowan and Derryveagh Mountains, with Slieve Snaght in the foreground, and the lower ranges on this side of Dunlewy, and the white peak of Arrigal peering loftily behind. "In fact, if the weather is fine—and it all depends on that—there is scarce such another mountain view in the kingdom."† To the left are the Crohy Hills, subsiding here into low ridges with nothing striking in their conformation, along which the road is carried to

DUNGLOE, "a dreary looking village on the side of a hill, which rises rather sharply from the water's side."‡ It is situated at the head of a rather wide inlet of the sea, guarded on the outside by the island of Inishfree. The water is so shallow that it is not a fit station even for the smallest boats. At the foot of the town is a brawling mountain torrent,

* Murray.   † Ibid.   ‡ Ibid.

which in rainy weather rushes down its rocky bed with a deafening roar. The only noticeable piece of architecture in the place is the Catholic chapel, which is a spacious building, and is furnished with a handsome marble altar.

I.—Excursion to Crohy Head.

The tourist should make an excursion to Crohy Head, for the sake of the view, which may be got from that point, of the extensive district of Temple-crone. The distance is but four miles, the road running along the shore as far as the martello tower. The elevation of the Head is not more than 800 feet. Northward you look on a singular stretch of coast—a seaboard dotted with rocks and lakelets, and a coast-line marvellously irregular, presenting a perfect chaos of land and water, and a multitude of islands, looking, to borrow Thackeray's image, like dolphins playing in the bay. "To the south-west, overlooking Gweebarra Bay, is a singular land-slip, called by the inhabitants '*Tholla Bristha*,' (broken earth.) The rocks seem to have been shaken and shivered to pieces—in fact, macadamized on a prodigious scale, and present an awfully shattered appearance. The chasm varies in its dimensions, the greatest gash being twelve feet wide above, and upwards of twenty-five deep. At some places the edges accurately correspond, and are serrated."* There is a fine range of precipices on the south-west side of the Head, and there is some good cave scenery, accessible only by a boat. The sportsman will find plenty of wild fowl and seal shooting on the coast, and trout fishing in the open loughs in the neighbourhood of Dungloe.

II.—Excursion to Burton Port and the Islands.

At the end of the second mile the road passes Meenmore Lough, near which there is an old, disused barrack, and two miles farther on, you reach Burton Port, which is the chief point of connexion between the islands of this coast and the mainland. Here are Roshin Lodge, (Mrs Foster,) and Lackbeg House, (G. Sproule, Esq.) Within a quarter of an hour's rowing is "*Rutland Island*, where, during the Lord Lieutenancy of the Duke of Rutland in 1785, £40,000 was expended in making a military station and general emporium for this part of the country."† The island is now a mere sandbank; about a dozen of small dwelling-houses remain, the sand has destroyed all the rest.

Off Rutland is Arranmore, a large island, on which there are some eighty families. If the tourist is

* Donegal Tourist, *apud* Murray. † Murray.

fond of boating, and is not pressed for time, he may have an abundantly interesting day's excursion in fine weather in exploring its cave and cliff scenery, which is very fine, particularly in the neighbourhood of the lighthouse, and indeed all round the north-west side of the island.

About a mile north of Burton Port is Castle Port, accessible only to the pedestrian, where once stood Dungloe Castle. "Murray's Handbook" notes here that there still remains the isolated ruin of the castle; the present writer has been in the locality more than once, but has not seen the ruin alluded to.

From Burton Port the pedestrian, wishing to go to Gweedore, may follow the by-road passing Kadu strand, and on to Kincaslagh, where there is a Catholic chapel, a spacious and well-built edifice; thence to Mullaghderg, where there is a considerable lake, separated only by a sand-bank from the sea. Out on the coast are one of those martello towers, and a rock, called the Spanish Rock, from the circumstance of a wreck of a Spanish vessel, supposed to have belonged to the Armada, having occurred there. In the memory of the inhabitants of this parish, " a number of well-finished brass guns were fished up, but unfortunately got into the hands of some travelling tinkers, by whose advice they were speedily broken up, and sold to themselves, of course

at a fabulous profit." Off the coast, a little to the
north, is a group of rocks, called the Stags, which,
according to a legend told in the district, had once
upon a time been a fleet of seven magnificent ships
belonging to that order of beings known as "gentle
folk," but were changed by some powerful enchan-
tress into ocean rocks. After a period of years
they are allowed to resume the form they had at
the moment in which they were metamorphosed, and
they are then allowed to sail away, under the condition that they are seen by no human eye. It is
needless to add, that the moment of emancipation
for the unfortunate Stags has invariably arrived
when the eyes of some man were directed towards
them. Some twenty years ago—as it was told to
the writer—an old man living in the neighbourhood
of Annagray saw seven ships in full sail setting
from the shore. It was a beautiful evening about
midsummer; the ships were of immense size, and
their rigging gorgeous; the sails were of silk, resembling the rich colour of a cloud in the setting
sun, while streamers of the same colour floated from
every mast; the decks were alive with busy crews,
dressed in caps and jackets of bright red. The old
man gazed on the sight for a moment in rapt admi-
ration, when presently the beautiful sails collapsed,
gathering the entire rigging into thick folds, like an

umbrella quickly shut; and when he rubbed his eyes hard and looked again, the beautiful vision had vanished, and nothing was seen but the Stags pointing their sharp heads up from the blue waters. He then recollected how he had often ridiculed the story of their enchantment, but now he doubted it no more. From Mullaghderg the pedestrian may keep along the coast to the place called the Point, where he will easily find a boat to take him across to Bunbeg, and proceed thence to the Gweedore Hotel.

The direct road from Dungloe to Gweedore (thirteen miles) traverses a flat moor, for the most part desolate, but relieved in fine weather by the mountain ranges that bound the view to the right, and the broken coast away to the left, both which prospects have already been noticed. At Lough Anure there is work for the geologist. "The environs consist of mica slate, with coarse granular dolomite. . . . . On one spot will be found basilar idiocrase and epidote, crystallised in six-sided prisms, with common garnet of a reddish-brown colour."* At the head of Annagray creek the solitude is broken by a hamlet, which is graced by a police-barrack and a national school; and a little farther on, "the Gweedore river is crossed at a spot where a combination of rock and waterfall offers charming scenery."† From

---

* Giesecke, *apud* Murray.   † Murray.

hence the road runs over a bleak moorland to Gweedore Hotel.

GLENTIES TO GWEEDORE.

The usual route between Glenties and Gweedore is through Dungloe, and this is the more direct road. But there is a far better route passing through the valleys of Lough Finn, Lough Barra, and Lough Beagh, or Lough Veagh, all which would be lost to the passing tourist who should follow the beaten track, though in all the more striking characteristics of Highland scenery they surpass anything in Donegal. The proposed route is thirty-nine miles, while that by Dungloe is thirty, but a difference of nine miles will not, one should suppose, weigh much against the pomp of lofty mountain, deep lake, headlong torrent, and topling precipice. The great, in fact the only, inconvenience of this route is the absence of hotels on the way; it will be necessary, therefore, to take a car, and to start early. The Dungloe route, just traced, may be explored by special excursion from Gweedore.

Leaving Glenties, the road takes a north-easterly direction, following the valley of the Shallagan river, and having on the left the Derryloghan mountains, and Aghla on the right. After the third mile, a road is given off to the left, which leads to Ducarry by the right bank of the Gweebarra.* The tourist will be careful to keep the Fintown road, skirting Knockrawer, which looks from a distance like a gigantic pyramid. At the fifth mile he gains the watershed ; and following for a short distance a gentle incline, comes suddenly on Lough Finn, a narrow strip of water extending some three or four miles from south-west to north-west. On the right rises the immense mass of Aghla (1961 ft.) sheer from the water, and the threatening steep, clothed with dark heath and torn by mountain torrents, gives the place an air of wild grandeur. Still, the scene is not savage, for there are plots of cultivated ground on the margin of the lake. There is a legend that a giant called *Fear-Gowan*, one of the famous Fenian heroes, perished on the bank of this lake. The story goes, that the *Fear-Gowan*, who had his principal residence at Glenlehin, some six miles to the north-west, returning from a visit in the south of Ireland, approached the haunt of a wild-boar that had long ruled supreme in the mountains south of Lough Finn, and had come off victorious from many a bloody encounter with the bravest Fenian huntsmen. The *Fear-Gowan* was young, but had an elder sister of the true Fenian stamp, who advised him strongly to keep clear of this formidable boar, and his friends

* See Excursion from Glenties to Dungloe, page 152.

the Fenians "up the country" gave him similar advice. But it was the rule with this youth, says the story, to do exactly the reverse of whatever he was advised to do. He was proud of his own prowess, and had with him three dogs which he fancied were invincible. Accordingly he sought the monster in his den, which was situated on a hillock near the head of the Glenmore, about three miles from the modern Glenties. The encounter began here, and was continued by the heads of the glens on towards Lough Finn. Confident that any one of his dogs should be a match for the boar, the Fear-Gowan first slipped one, which after a bloody struggle was left dead on the moor. He then let loose a second, which was killed also ; and then his last and best dog was slipped to the contest, soon to be torn to pieces, like the others, by the infuriate animal, which now attacked the giant himself. The Fear-Gowan bravely defended himself, retreating the while over mountain and moor, till at length the combatants, struggling down the steep sides of Aghla, were brought to a stand on the eastern bank of Lough Finn. The boar was proving too many for the giant, who now began to shout lustily for his sister, and his great voice shook the mountains for miles around. The sister heard him, and came speedily over the hills towards Lough

L

Finn, filling her apron as she advanced with large stones that lay along her path. By the time she reached Lough Finn her brother and the boar were both prostrate. He was able to call, but, owing to the echoes of the mountains, she mistook the point whence the shouts proceeded. At a place where the lake was not deep she waded across, but when she got to the other side the voice seemed to come from the side she had left, and when she returned, the voice again seemed to issue from the opposite side ; and thus was she kept crossing and re-crossing that luckless lake, till at last the cries of her brother becoming fainter and fainter, and the echoes gradually dying out, she succeeded in reaching the spot. There lay the boar dead on the ground, and near it the Fear-Gowan, a mass of torn flesh. The sister, exhausted by her wild efforts to relieve her brother and her anguish of mind, sank down beside him, and both died about the same moment. Her name was Finna ; hence the name of Lough Finn.

The eighth mile brings the tourist to Finntown, "a small village beautifully situated on the banks of Lough Finn,"* where a Catholic chapel, resting on a slope that rises from the water's edge, a police barrack and a few cottages, with a piece of young plantation, make altogether a fine Highland picture.

* Murray.

On the opposite side of the lake rise the steep cliffs of Scraigs, (1410 feet,) bare and weather-beaten. This lake is the source of the river Finn, which flows eastward by Ballyboffey and Stranorlar, where it spreads into a beautiful river, and uniting with the Mourne at Lifford, flows on to Derry.

From Finntown to Ducarry the distance is four miles, and the road abounds in all the incident of rocky defile, steep hill, and mountain tarn. Ducarry possesses many attractions both for the general tourist and for the angler, but it lacks that one indispensable attraction of every such resort, an hotel. Here is the fishery depot of the Gweebarra, which is a good salmon fishery. The tide comes up to this place.

From Ducarry the road follows the course of the Owenwee river up the valley of the Gweebarra, which soon becomes a fine mountain pass. The sixth mile from Ducarry brings you into the lone region of Lough Barra. The lough itself is a small sheet of placid water, black as ink, with a margin of beautiful golden sand, contrasting finely with the dark waters of the lake. Two torrents, one of which is called Schruhan-Crolee, and the other Scardangle, come headlong down the steep side of Slieve Snaght, forming two pretty waterfalls, which are visible from the road, and may easily be approached.

If the visitor be a fair pedestrian, he may enjoy a few hours' exciting mountaineering by ascending Slieve Snaght, which is more easily climbed than Errigal, and affords almost the same marvellous wealth of prospect far and wide. He should keep along the crest of the mountains, a pathless course on which the history of many a storm is written, till he stands over the Poisoned Glen, the view of which will amply repay him for the fatigue of the excursion. It is a deep vale, guarded by frowning precipices, so savage and so lonely that the visitor is not likely soon to forget this wild mountain recess. On the right, Glenveagh lies beneath his feet, and the tourist should now descend to regain the road in the valley.

From Lough Barra the road ascends between Slieve Snaght and Crockbrack till the watershed is reached, and then descends into Glenbeagh,* or Glenveagh, the road to the right leading to Letter- kenny. The tourist may here consult his map with advantage, for from this point he will gain a clear idea of the physical arrangement of the Highland district of Donegal. The great pass that traverses Donegal from the Gweebarra to the Mulroy Bay is now, to a great extent, under his eye. Almost parallel to this is the vale from Glenties up to

* Properly Glen Beagha, *i.e.*, the glen of the birch trees.

Finntown.   On the southern side of the Glendowan range on his right is the valley in which repose the waters of the beautiful Gartan Lough, and again behind the Derryveagh range on his left is the pass opening on Gweedore, both nearly parallel to Glenveagh.   As you begin to descend your attention is attracted by glimpses of the narrow strip of water, "still and deep," enclosed between the precipitous sides of the Derryveagh and Glendowan mountains, like the "deep Trossach,"

"So wondrous wild, the whole might seem
The scenery of a fairy dream."*

On the left are Staghall, (1599,) then Croagh-na-Saggart, then Dooish, (2147,) the highest point in the whole range, and further down is Saggart-na-Dooish, ending with Kingarrow at the entrance of the glen below.   On the right are Farscallop, Kinnaveagh, (1270,) and Altachoastia, (1737.)   The eagle still frequents this wild region.   At the head of the lake are a police-barrack and a cottage, "the residence of J. Adair, Esq., whose proceedings in the eviction of his tenants obtained considerable and somewhat unenviable notoriety."†

The Rev. Cæsar Otway has left the following sketch of Glenveagh :—"We proceeded to Glen-

* Scott.   † Murray.

veagh, and at length reached it after a very deep descent. We were delighted with the beautiful water, winding far between immense mountains, and apparently without end, losing itself in gloom and solitariness amidst the distant gorges and defiles of the hills. On the right hand side of the lake the mountain rises like a steep wall out of the water, lofty and precipitous for a thousand feet; and this cliff is the secure eyrie of the eagle and jer-falcon. On the other side the shore was lofty also, and mountainous; but still there was room for the oak and the birch, the rowan and the alder, to strike their roots amidst the rock, and clothe the ravines and hollows with ornamental copse-wood. The lake itself is studded with wet woody islands,* out of which rose perpendicular columns of smoke, which told full well that in this solitary secluded spot the illicit distiller was at his tempting and hazardous work. I have never been in Switzerland or Scotland; it has not been my lot at leisure to wander along the waters of Westmoreland or Cumberland, but I have seen good drawings of these most frequented scenes; and have thus admired Loch Katrine, the subject of the poet's pen and painter's pencil. But if *my* glen and *my* lake were

* There is something of exaggeration in saying that it is "studded with islands."

not Irish, if the curse of being out of fashion did
not put everything Irish under attainder, I would
venture to show Glenveagh against any of those
foreign fashionables, and would encourage my mountain nymph to hold herself as fair in varied beauty
as any of them.   .   .   .   .   .   .

"I cannot take leave of Glenveagh without calling
to mind a visit we paid to a characteristic dweller
of this singular and solitary scene. In a sunny
nook, where a dark, deep ravine expanded itself
into a little grassy valley, affording room for a
potato garden and a small meadow, and beside a
small garrulous brook, rose a cabin, I dare not call
it a cottage, for that supposes comfort, and associates cleanliness, neatness, the woodbine bower,
the rose-covered lattice, with its idea, and such a
spot on Ulleswater or Windermere would have been
blessed and beautified with such accompaniments;
but here we had no such amenities, the grunt of
a sleeping sow, the growl of a gaunt greyhound,
were the sounds that accosted us as we bent our
heads to enter the narrow aperture that served
almost as much for a chimney as an entrance.
But when you entered, things bore somewhat a
more satisfactory appearance; there was better furniture than is generally to be seen in an Irish cabin,
some old-fashioned high-backed chairs, some old,

carved, broken, brass-mounted chests; a decent
dresser, on which were ranged some pewter dishes
and plates; implements of fishing were suspended
along the walls, and a long French musket, its barrel
mounted with brass, hung right over the immense
mantelpiece of the chimney that jutted out almost
into the centre of the apartment; above the gun
was an old mezzotinto print of the Holy Family
after Raphael, and over that again on old armorial
bearing, on which you could observe a salmon, a
lion passant, and a bloody hand, all well smoked.
Beneath the canopy of the immense chimney, and
beside the hob, in a comfortable high-backed chair,
made of straw in the manner of a beehive, sat Jack
M'Swine, the master of the mansion. He rose apparently with pain as we entered. I thought he
would never cease rising, so slowly did he unbend
his extraordinary height, and with apparent difficulty, as suffering under rheumatic pains, he advanced to meet my friend, whom he accosted with
all the ease of an old gentleman, and all the cordi-
ality of an ancient Irishman. All the humbler class
of Irish are particularly civil and attentive to you
when you enter their houses. I never in any of
the provinces entered under a poor man's roof, that
I was not received with the smile of pleasure and
the language of benignity, the best seat wiped, and

offered for my acceptance, the pig expelled, the dog punished if he dared to growl at my entering; but here was even something better than this, for there was the Irish heartiness adorned with the urbanity of a gentleman; if he were the lord of a palace he could not have received us with more kind and unembarrassed courtesy, than did this dweller of the lonely mountain hut; and when I was introduced to him as one who came from Dublin to see and admire the beauties of Glenveagh, nothing could exceed the anxious kindness with which he expressed his desire to do everything to further my views; he lamented he had not a boat, that his fowling convenience and fishing-tackle were not in trim for our use; in short, he seemed to feel a double pang that he was a poor man. But who was Jack M'Swine? The lineal descendant of the ancient sept of the M'Swines, who, next and only inferior to the O'Donnell, preserved a large portion of Tirconnell. Our friend of Glenveagh maintained that he was the M'Swine-na-Doo—the Caunfinny, or head of the family. And surrounded by poverty as we saw him, the dweller of the wretched hut, without one shilling of income, with nothing to live on but the produce of his potato garden, and the milk of a few cows that ranged the mountains, yet Philip the Second of Spain, ruling over dominions on which the sun never set, was not prouder in his bearing, nor richer in the recollections of his Austrian ancestry, than this fading shadow of an Irish Tanist : the man literally lived, moved, and had his being as dependent on his family associations; and still life was only supportable under the one hope which he cherished.   Amidst chilling discouragements, insurmountable obstacles, and endless rebuffs, he had now come to the verge of the grave ; gray he stood and tempest worn, like one of the withering oaks on the side of Glenveagh, and still he put forth the leaf and struggled for existence, hoping against hope.   The M'Swines, as proprietors of a large portion of the mountain district of Donegal, had usually sided with the O'Neils against the O'Donnells ; and O'Neil's demand of sixty cows as tribute from O'Donnell was often enforced by the assistance of M'Swine ; and when James I. conquered the O'Donnells, and escheated their lands, as a reward to M'Swine for his opposition to this chieftain, his mountains, perhaps because not worth confiscating, were left him in peace ; and in the following reign of Charles, when the execrable rebellion of 1641 broke out, the M'Swine for some reason did not join it.   There was no proof of massacre or murder against him, and the Act of Settlement left him his property as an innocent Papist.

Here, then, down to the present century, the M'Swines lived the lords paramount of these glens and mountains, in barbarous and profuse hospitality. Here, surrounded by followers and retainers, amidst fosterers and cosherers, their hall full of horse boys, dog boys, and cow boys,—all idlers, all gentlemen, all disdaining any trade or occupation,— fishing, fowling, hunting, or fighting by day; feasting, quarrelling, and carousing by night—the M'Swines, from father to son, lived: borrowing money, and mortgaging one mountain tract, or line of sea, after another. This is the common history of an Irish Castle-Rack-rent family; and thus the common fate of the Sir Thadys and Sir Condys of Ireland attended the M'Swines, and our poor friend, Jack, came into the world the inheritor of his fore-father's name, pride, recollections, and imprudences; but, alas! his lands had all vanished, and became, under foreclosed mortgages, the properties of families who possessed the low-born English and Scotch propensity of foresight and frugality. Still Jack M'Swine clung to the hope and expectation of re-covering some of his alienated lands; he told us how certain tracts were illegally conveyed away from him by his father, and he besought me, with all the anxiety of a man who was catching at vague impossibilities, that I would search the records of

Dublin Castle for him, and make out his title. No one could possibly have seen this fine old man, so tall, so meagre, and yet so decent in his coarse attire, and so urbane and gracious in the old-fashioned manner of the last century, without wishing that some portion of the wide domains of his ancestors was restored to him, and that his gray hairs might descend in decency to the grave ; or rather it would better become my desire, and my prayer, to turn these immoderate hopes, these ceaseless anxieties from such unreal fancies, from these fallacies of earthly ambition, to seek a property in a better country—an inheritance with the saints in light—desiring to be found in Christ, clothed in His righteousness, endowed with His unspeakable gifts, and possessing His unsearchable riches. Every year this hearty old Milesian comes down from his mountain glen and spends a day at the hospitable glebe-house of my friend, and he regularly brings to the younger part of the family an appropriate present; a gift which, from the remotest times, a king might accept, and a noble might bestow—a young eagle or jer-falcon of the true hunting breed, from the cliffs of Glenveagh. Before I left the country, this genuine gentleman brought me such a present as a grateful recompense (the only one he could bestow), for the hearty interest and attention which I, as he said, condescended to take in the fallen fortunes of poor John M'Swine." *

A short distance below the cottage is Glenleck, a hollow in the mountain side, down which a brawling torrent tumbles, in a channel concealed under a dense copse. The visitor will find a path by which he can ascend the ravine through the heath, which here grows to great perfection. The place gives forth charming echoes ; a gun fired from a boat at certain points of the lake is answered by a loud crashing noise as of the mountains falling to pieces. It is a pity there is not here a boat which the passing visitor might hire for an hour. It is a pity, too, that the road passing through the glen is not cared for by the gentlemen of the Grand Jury of Donegal. This road, oftentimes sorely in need of repair, borders the lake, which is between three and four miles long, all the way down to the lower end, where it joins the direct road between Letterkenny and Gweedore. Here the Owencarrow river, flowing from Lough-veagh, in the same north-easterly direction, on to Glen Lough, thence to the sandy shores of Ros-gul, is crossed at Glenveagh bridge, where there is a police barrack. The road now trends to the west, skirting Kingarrow, and leaving Muckish (2214 feet) to the right, remarkable for its elongated

* Sketches in Donegal.

crest and fine escarpment, ascends the valley of the
Culabber, a singularly wild Highland vale. On the
left is the great Dooish range, already seen from
Glenveagh, while on the right are Crocknalaragh
(1554 feet), Aghla-beg (1860 feet), Aghla-mor (1916
feet), and " peering loftily over the very end of the
valley is the singular and beautiful summit of Errigal (2466 feet), with its glistening seams of quartz.
As the traveller ascends towards the watershed, he
gains charming peeps of Glen Lough in the foreground, while near the summit level, the attention
is arrested on the right by Altan Lough, a dark,
savage-looking tarn, in a deep gap between Aghla-
mor and Errigal, both of which mountains slope
down to its banks with great rapidity."* When
" the watershed is gained, a view opens up, which
is hardly to be surpassed in Great Britain."† Before you is the beautiful mountain valley of Dunlewey, enlivened by some white houses and cottages,
amongst which the school-house and police barrack are conspicuous. In the middle of the valley
lies the lake, whose glassy surface is broken by a
few islands, covered with ash trees. On its banks
is built a handsome church of pure white marble,
which is found here in great abundance, and a
little beyond, on a wooded slope rising from the
water, is Dunlewey House, (Mrs Russell's.) To the

* Murray.   † Idem.

left is the Poisoned Glen, a dark defile ending above
in a fine range of precipices, that rise like mural
battlements around. Hugging the steep base of
Errigal, the road is carried by Dunlewy Lough
and Lough Nacung, and on by the Clady river
to the Gweedore Hotel. This well appointed
hotel, with its surroundings of green sward and
bright leafage of young trees, and other pleasant
amenities, making an oasis in the midst of the un-
tamed wilderness, reminds one of how much might
have been done, and how little has been done, for
the unrivalled scenery of the Donegal Highlands.
The tourist will feel grateful to Lord George Hill,
who has provided the present comfortable hostelry,
and for the rest must be content with a hope that
other landed proprietors will follow his example in
this particular.

Here is a capital station for the angler. There is
good fishing on the Clady and the fresh water loughs;
and what is a source of infinite satisfaction to the
casual visitor, the manager of the hotel is empowered
to give leave to any gentleman staying there to fish,
under certain fair conditions.

Distances.—Dungloe, 13 miles; Dunlooey, 6
miles; Crossroads, 10 miles; Dunfanaghy, 17 miles.

I. EXCURSION TO ERRIGAL.

The tourist should not omit to make an excursion

to the top of Errigal. He may have a car to the foot of the mountain, about six miles from the hotel ; and, as Errigal rises rapidly, the ascent may be made in two hours. The path is in great part over a shingly surface, consisting mainly of loose stones, of a pure white colour, which make this beautiful sugar-loaf look from the distance like a snow-capped Alp, to which circumstance, probably, it owes its name, which may mean " The White Peak." The footing is not exactly precarious ; but there is need of caution near the top, where the acclivity narrows to an edge, with yawning depths on either side. When you have reached the summit, which is only a few feet across, you command a prospect of land and sea such as might satisfy an eagle's circle of vision. " Oh for a clear day ! " Looking downward you feel yourself circled by abysses so deep, so silent, that it takes you a time to realize that your watch-tower is built on a solid foundation. To the south, over against you, rises Slieve Snaght, seeming so near that you fancy you could step on it, and linked to it are the summits of the Derryveagh range, a savage region, bare and desolate ; and close behind, a throng of mountain tops, receding in a tumultuous sea, southward still, as far as Benbulben and the other ranges of northern Connaught. And with these are linked the forms of many mountains of the counties of Tyrone and Derry, crowding the horizon away to the distant Knocklayde in the north-east of Antrim ; more to the north are seen the hills of Caledonia looming afar off,

" Like the bright confines of another world."*

Then a low azure ridge cuts even against the sky : there is no mistaking it; it is the ocean, and your eyes come quickly homeward over its unbroken field till they rest on the headlands of Inishowen and Fanad, and the shores of Lough Foyle and Lough Swilly, and the broken coast of Mulroy, and, nearer still, the solitary Torry. The western coast lies at your feet. Beneath is Gweedore spread out like a leaf, and the sixteen quarter lands of Rosses, a rocky region, where, from the multitude of its lakelets, one would imagine land and water were left still commingled in original chaos, and then an array of islands, the chief of which are Gola, and Owey, and Cruit, and Arran, which looks a mountain from the plain below ; but, seen from this lofty peak, it lies a stretch of quiet lowland. Inland, you peep into a thousand and one valleys that have in this mountain—the symbol of a higher unity—a common friend and centre through whom they hold communion with each other. An impressive spec-

* Wordsworth.

M

tacle truly, the whole of the wide circle visible from this pinnacle! and, if it shows not "the kingdoms of the earth and the glory of them," it speaks a higher revelation;—it reveals the Infinite, and surely inspires sober thought and deepest reverence.

II. EXCURSION TO DUNGLOE.

This excursion has been traced above, under *Excursion from Dungloe to Gweedore.**

GWEEDORE TO DUNFANAGHY AND LETTERKENNY.

Leaving the Gweedore Hotel the road for some seven or eight miles traverses a wild and desolate moorland, with Errigal on the right, and on the left Bloody Foreland, a bold headland (1000 feet) stretching away into the sea, and distinguished by one of those martello towers which abound on the northwest coast of Donegal. After crossing the Tullughobegly river, green fields and little hamlets begin to enliven the landscape. Bedlam is a characteristic bit of a village, beyond which is the Catholic Chapel, and near it, conspicuous in a field above, is the pretty and hospitable residence of the parish priest (Rev. H. M'Fadden.) A little farther on, passing the Protestant rectory, charmingly situated at the

* Page 152.

head of Ballyness Bay, north of which is a group of islands, viz., Innishbofin, Inishdooey, and Inishbeg, you arrive at

FALCARRAGH, or Cross Roads, a small village occupying an exposed situation on the northern coast, and commanding a fine view of the mountains inland. The geologist may find interesting occupation in exploring the tideways to the north-west, as there are striking indications of a subsidence of the coast in that quarter. Lying out by itself in the midst of the vast blue field of ocean, Torry Island, its rocks rising tower-like from the waves, fixes itself on the attention of the traveller. Falcarragh is a good point from whence to make excursions to Muckish mountain, and to Torry, for which excursions Dunfanaghy also may be made a convenient starting point.

I. EXCURSION TO MUCKISH.

Beyond Falcarragh a road branches off to the right, running up to Muckish Gap, which is the easiest approach to Muckish (Pig's Back), a mountain that will well repay the tourist for the trouble of an excursion. The ascent is fatiguing. " The geological structure consists of a very thin slaty mica, and granular quartz, and silver-white mica. At the height of 500 feet is an extensive bed of white quartz sand, in very minute grains, which has been exported to the glass-works of Dumbarton, being considered an excellent material."* The summit, which looks a sharp linear ridge from the distance, is a flat stretch, well covered with moss and peculiar grasses, amongst which the pretty saxifrage (London Pride) abounds. The view is wondrous fine of earth and ocean, but as it is pretty nearly the same as that seen from Errigal's lofty summit, it is only necessary here to note, in addition to the outline traced from that point, that the shores of Sheep-haven are now under your feet.

II. Excursion to Torry Island.

Torry † is some eight miles distant from the coast. It is a desolate island, nearly three miles in length, very narrow, and affording but a very small area capable of producing crop of any kind. "The rock scenery of its coast is very fine and character-istic. Porphyritic syenite appears to be the geolo-gical structure."‡ But its chiefest attractions are for the antiquary. In remote pagan times, it was one of the main strongholds of the Fomorians, one of whose chiefs erected a tower on a cliff at the eastern extremity of the island, called Tor-Connaing, celebrated in our pre-Christian annals as

* Giescke.
† Sometimes written Tory, Torree, Torry, Innis-Torry.
‡ Murray.

" The Tower of the Island, the Island of the Tower,
The citadel of Connaing, the son of Toelar." *

Here was fought a famous battle, in which the fierce tribes of those early days maintained the conflict on the strand at Port Doon till the returning tide buried nearly all the combatants in the waves. Here the formidable "Balor of the mighty blows" had his head-quarters. This Balor is still vividly remembered in the traditions of Torry Island, where a very curious story is told of him, which Dr O'Donovan, in his learned edition of the Annals of the Four Masters, deemed worthy of a special notice. The story runs thus:—In days of yore there lived three brothers, Gavida, MacSamthaim, and MacKineely, the first of whom was a distinguished smith, who kept his forge at Drunnatinnè, a place in the parish of Rath-Finan. MacKineely was lord of that district, comprising the parishes of Rath-Finan and Tullaghobegly, and owned a cow called *Glas Gaivlen,* so lactiferous as to be greatly coveted by the neighbours. At this period Torry Island was governed by a famous captain, called Balor, who had one eye in the middle of his forehead, and another directly opposite it in the back of his skull. This latter eye, like that of the basilisk, had a mortiferous power, and was kept constantly closed by Balor, except when he wished to de-

* The Book of Leacan.

stroy an adversary with it. A Druid had prophesied that Balor should be murdered by his own grandson. To nullify this prediction, he shut up his only child, a daughter, in an impregnable tower built on the summit of Tormore, a cliff on the north-east of the island, under the keeping of twelve matrons, whom he strictly charged to keep her not only from intercourse with, but even from the knowledge of the existence of the male sex. Time passed, and Ethnea grew into a beautiful woman. Balor, now apparently secure against the prediction of the Druid, at the head of an adventurous band of sea-rovers, swept the neighbouring coast from the sea, but his ambition could not be satisfied unless with the possession of the Glas Gaivlen. One day, the MacKineely above-mentioned, having had occasion to go to his brother's forge to get some swords made, took with him the Glas Gaivlen on a halter. Arrived at the forge, he entrusted the cow to his brother MacSamthain, who was there too on a similar errand. While Mac-Kineely was within, Balor, in the form of a little red-haired boy, came to MacSamthain, and told him that he had just heard his two brothers saying, inside the forge, that they would use all his (Mac-Samthain's) steel in making MacKineely's swords. MacSamthain, deceived by the boy, gave the cow in charge to his little red-haired friend, and rushed into the forge. Balor, taking advantage of his opportunity, carried off the Glas Gaivlen to Torry Island, and the place on which he dragged her up on the island is to this day called Port-na-Glaise, or the harbour of the green cow. MacKineely, suspecting that a fraud had been practised on his brother by Balor, ran out of the forge, when lo! he saw the Fomorian chief and the cow in the middle of the sound of Torry. Grieved to distraction at the loss of his Glas Gaivlen, he made known his case to a friendly Druid living not far from the place. The Druid told him that the cow was irrecoverable as long as Balor lived, as he should keep his basilisk eye always open to destroy any one who dared approach her. Accordingly, MacKineely set about compassing the destruction of this fatal eye, and for this purpose called to his aid his familiar sprite, " Biroge of the mountain." She dressed him in the robes of a young girl, and wafting him across the sound to the tower of Ethnea, where, by representing her ward as a noble lady just rescued from a tyrant who attempted to carry her off, she succeeded in introducing MacKineely to Ethnea, who immediately became enamoured of him. The result of this intercourse was, that in due time Ethnea gave birth to three sons, whom Balor secured at once, and rolling them up in a sheet, fastened with a *delg*, or pin,

sent them in a boat to be consigned to the deep.
The *delg*, or pin, gave way as the boat crossed the
harbour, when one of the children fell into the water
and disappeared ;—the other two were drowned at
a spot which is, from this circumstance, called Port-
a-delg.   The child that had fallen out and disappeared was invisibly carried away, by the Banshee,
" Biroge of the mountain," to his father on the mainland, who sent him to his brother Gavida, to be
brought up to his trade, which in those days ranked
among the most respectable professions.

Balor, hearing how MacKineely had deceived and
injured him, crossed the Sound with a band of his
fierce associates, and landing at a place called Bally-
connell, succeeded in taking him ; and laying his
head on a large white stone, cut it clean off with one
blow of his ponderous sword.   This stone with its
red veins still tells of this deed of blood, and gives its
name to the present district of Cloghaneely.   It may
be seen now in the grounds of W. Olpherts, Esq.,
who has carefully placed it on a pillar six feet high.
The heir of MacKineely had in the meantime grown
up to be an able man and an excellent smith.   Fully
aware of the circumstances of his birth, and escape,
and his father's cruel death, he meditated revenge.
This he at length realized, for Balor one day came
to the forge, when the young MacKineely was alone

working, and happened, in the course of conversation to allude with pride to his victory over Mac-Kineely, never suspecting that he spoke to his son. The young smith, fired with rage, watched his opportunity, and taking a glowing rod from the furnace thrust it through the basilisk eye of Balor, thus amply avenging his father's death and fulfilling the prediction of the Druid.

St Collum Cille founded a monastery on this solitary island, which continued to flourish through a long lapse of ages down till Queen Elizabeth's governor of Connaught, the cruel Bingham, made a descent upon the place and destroyed everything that he could not carry away with him. A round tower, called the Clog-teach, "The Bell-House," still stands here, wanting a portion of the roof, and the foundations of a series of seven little churches or cells can still be traced with the aid of the traditions of the place. A few years ago, the Rev. J. M'Fadden, to whose parish Torry is attached, built there a pretty chapel, and enclosed the ancient graveyard with a strong wall. There are also a national school and a lighthouse on the island. The inhabitants, consisting of between seventy and eighty families, live altogether by fishing and kelp-making, sources of income sufficiently precarious.

The road from Falcarragh to Dunfanaghy turns

inland, crossing the Ray river near the old Myrath churchyard, where there is a gigantic cross made of one block of stone by St Collum Cille. It is now lying on the ground, and is broken in two places. It is told that the saint hewed the stone out of the side of Muckish mountain, at a place called Bally-na-cross, and that, owing to his prayer, angels carried it from that place to old Myrath. Four miles further on the road cuts off the peninsula of Horn Head, and enters Dunfanaghy, "a neat little town with a very fair hotel, whence the traveller can comfortably make his excursions to the scenery of Horn Head."*

EXCURSION TO HORN HEAD.

"The view from Horn Head is one *per se*, and should not be omitted by the northern traveller in Ireland."† Shortly after leaving Dunfanaghy the road crosses a narrow channel, through which the tide rushes, thus insulating Horn Head. A little beyond is Horn Head House, the residence of the Rev. C. Stewart, the Protestant rector of this parish, but the guide will turn to the left and lead you over the sandhills to M'Swine's Gun, which is a marine cave, in whose roof there is an orifice open to the surface above. In times of storm, the sea dashing into the cave rushes upwards with great force, ac-

* Murray.   † Ibid.

companied by a loud explosion resembling the boom of a discharged piece of ordnance. The report, it is said, has been heard so far away as Derry. The M'Swines were the former lords of this district, and hence the name of this striking natural phenomenon. The visitor should keep close to the precipices towards the north-east, where there is a circular castle, near which is Horn Head proper, viz., a cliff projecting somewhat in the shape of a horn. Here the cliffs rise 800 feet sheer from the water. The Rev. C. Otway has left a lively sketch of these cliffs. "Did Shakespeare see these enormous battlements of Ireland? Dover Cliff, of which he gives such a sublime description, is perhaps magnified in the imagery of the poet; but certainly, I conceive Horn Head comes up to his representation. One would think the Muse had caught up from Stratford-upon-Avon the poet of nature, and dropt him on this mighty promontory, until he had made up in his mind's eye the whole magnificent scene.

> ' How fearful
> And dizzy 'tis to cast one's eyes so low !
> The crows and choughs that wing the midway air,
> Show scarce so gross as beetles : half way down
> Hangs one that gathers samphire ; dreadful trade !
> Methinks he seems no bigger than his head ;
> The fishermen that walk upon the beach
> Appear like mice ; and yon tall anchoring bark
> Diminished to her cock ; her cock a buoy
> Almost too small for sight. The murmuring surge

That on unnumbered idle pebbles chafes,
Cannot be heard so high—I 'll look no more.'

Nothing, indeed, could be more astonishing than the whole scene ; there was a mist hanging over the Atlantic, that gave a mysteriousness to its magnificence, like the way into the eternal world—shadows, clouds, and darkness rested upon it ; there was no wind, it was a perfect calm, and yet the roll of the waves, and the roar of the tides, as they rushed and rolled amidst the caverned cliffs, communicated an awful grandeur to the whole scene. It was the moan of suffering endurance under the ceaseless exertion of the Atlantic. . . . Now, in the midst of July, if it was a scene pregnant with grandeur, it was also one teeming with life."* "The student of natural history will fine plenty of ornithological interest amongst the various sea-birds that frequent these cliffs, amongst which are the shelldrake, *(Tudorna vulpauser,)* the guillamot, *(Uria troide,)* the sea parrot, the cormorant, the shag, *(Phalacrocorox,)* the gannot, the stormy petrel, the speckled diver *(Colymbus glacialis,)* and many others."† The view northward is one of boundless ocean ; to the north-west lies Torry, to the south-west the group Inishbeg, Inishdooey, and Inishboffin, and on the north-east the headlands of Northern Donegal,

* Sketches in Donegal.   † Murray.

viz., Melmore, Rinmore, Fanad, Dunaff, and Malin Heads, retiring in rugged perspective, while away in the distance is seen the little island of Inishtrahull. In fine weather it is an interesting excursion in a boat round the Head. The geologist will find much to interest him in the structure of the cliffs, and the sportsman will find shooting to his heart's content. The tourist needs not to be reminded of the influence of weather upon scenery of every kind. Horn Head, under every condition of atmosphere, offers effects of the most striking character. It looks most glorious, indeed, when lit up by the beams of the early sun ; but no matter at what hour of the day it is seen, no matter at what season, whether in sunshine or in cloud, in calm weather or in rough, the visitor will come away from the Horn —that beetling cliff, hanging some 800 feet above the sea—deeply impressed by the scene.

DUNFANAGHY TO LETTERKENNY.

The route now takes a south-easterly direction. On the right is the dark mass of Muckish, on the left, Sheephaven, of which charming views are obtained from different points of the road. At first, skirting the shore, the road passes the Seissagh Lough, a mile from Dunfanaghy, and, traversing hilly ground, touches at the Catholic Chapel of

Clondahorky two miles further on, where a road is given off to the left, leading to Ards House, (A. Stewart, Esq.,) situated on one of the inlets of Sheephaven, " which, with its extensive, beautiful woods and adjacent farm, is one of the most desirable places in the north of Ireland. The views, however, from this side of the haven are not so diversified or pleasant as they are from Rosapenna."* A mile and a quarter further on is Creeslough, a small village, situated on an upland between Muckish and the sea, in the neighbourhood of which is Doe Castle, a stronghold of the M'Swines, guarding the most southern inlet of Sheephaven. The fortress of former days is in our own a pleasant mansion, belonging to A. Maddison, Esq. The circular architecture of the keep or prison has preserved its external identity ; but, within, the grim visage of the gaoler has given place to the radiant face of the dairy-maid. Instead of a fosse guarded by frowning bastions, the visitor will find a few small pieces of ordnance reposing peacefully on a smiling lawn. It was in this neighbourhood that the famous Owen Roe O'Neil landed from Belgium in 1641. From this point there is a good view over the Sands of Rosapenna, where " a line of coast and country extends from the sea deep into the land . . . . exhi-

* Murray.

biting one wide waste of red sand ; for miles, not a blade of grass, not a particle of verdure, but hills and dales, and undulating swells, smooth, solitary, desolate, reflecting the sun from their polished surface of one uniform flesh-like hue. Fifty years ago, this line of coast was as highly improved in its way as Ards on the opposite side of the bay now is . . . . it contained the comfortable mansion of Lord Boyne, an old-fashioned manorial house and garden, planted ad laid out in the taste of that time, with avenues and terraces, hedges, and statues, surrounded with walled parks. . . . . But now not a vestige of this is to be seen—one common waste of sand—one undistinguished ruin covers all." *

" Beyond Rosapenna, at Downing's Bay, there is one of the finest views in Donegal, looking up and down Sheephaven, with the woods of Ards, and the tower of Doe Castle backed up in the distance by the ponderous mass of Muckish." †

Leaving Creeslough, the road traverses a tract of cold moorland, affording a magnificent panorama of mountains away to the right, embracing, besides Muckish, the Errigal group, the Dooish and the Glendowan ranges, while close on the left rises Lough Salt Mountain, (1546.) About three miles from Creeslough, the Owencarrow is crossed at a point

* Otway-Sketches in Donegal. † Murray.

about midway between Glenveagh and Glen Lough. The road now enters a long defile, called the Gap, or Barness, intersecting one of the outliners of Lough Salt Mountain. The sides of the Gap are rugged and precipitous, and near the top almost grand. On emerging from the pass, the road strikes into an open country gradually assuming a more cultivated character as you advance, and affording views, especially of the mountains away to the right, whi keep the attention constantly excited. Passing T mon Catholic Chapel, you drop into Kilmacrenan, poor village, but " very prettily situated in th mountain valley through which the Lannan river rushes down in picturesque stream." *

Kilmacrenan, or Cill'-Mac-Nenain, is remarkable as the foster-place of St Collum Cille,† and for an abbey founded here by the saint, which endured for many ages. It was the favourite ecclesiastical establishment of the O'Donnells, and the ruins still remain, " consisting of a slender and rather graceful tower, lighted by pointed windows, in the top stage, besides scanty remains of other buildings, surrounded by an enclosure. The parish church is said to have been built on the site of a Franciscan priory, and has over the door the sculptured head of an abbot taken from the abbey." ‡

* Murray.   † See Hist. Introd.   ‡ Murray.

Excursion to the Rock of Doon and Lough Salt.

At a short distance from Kilmacrenan is the Rock of Doon, " on which the O'Donnells were always inaugurated by priests, whom they regarded as descended from St Columb."* This is a rocky eminence, rising sharply from the ground—a splendid natural fortress in days when artillery was unknown. Amongst the many slanderous stories set forth by aldus Cambrensis, with no other view, one should ppose, than to asperse the Irish character, is an absurd account of the ceremony of inauguration of the chiefs of Tirconnell.† Lynch, a well-informed author — and there does not appear to be any reason to doubt his testimony—has left us the following description of the ceremony. He says, "That when the investiture (of the O'Donnell) took place at Cil-mhac-Crenain, he was attended by O'Ferghail, successor to Columbkille, and O'Galla-chius, his marshal, and surrounded by all the estates of the country. The Abbot O'Ferghail put a pure white, straight, unknotted rod into his hand, and said, 'Receive, sire, the auspicious ensign of your dignity, and remember to imitate in your government the whiteness, straightness, and unknottiness

---

* Lewis's Topograph. Dict.
† *Vide* Apologia pro Hibernia, p. 95.   Ed. 1849.

N

of this rod, to the end that no evil tongue may find cause to asperse the candour of your actions with blackness, nor any kind of corruption or tie of friendship be able to pervert your justice; therefore, in a lucky hour, take the government of this people, to exercise the power given you with freedom and security.'"* The story-tellers make Doon a head-quarters of the fairies: "There is a sort of cave in the eastern side of the rock, which forms a vestibule to an immense cavern, which is said to b within; this is the favourite abode of the *gooc people*, and their council-chamber. A thousand times troops of tiny people are seen entering the cave, and some gifted mortals have observed the door open, and have got a glimpse of sumptuous apartments and splendid banquetings within."† There is a tradition to the effect that Sir Cahir O'Doherty met his death on the Rock of Doon. Sir Cahir's history has all the elements that go to make up a popular hero. His youth, his handsome person, his devotion to the popular cause, and the early period put to his career, have gained him a place in the memory and imagination of most of his countrymen by the side of Hugh Roe and Robert Emmet. Near the Rock is a holy well, which the people hold in great veneration.

---

* *Apud* Otway's Sketches in Donegal.　　† Ibid.

Leaving the Rock of Doon, the tourist may return to the Kilmacrenan road, and ascend at once Lough Salt, a mountain which is the subject of one of Otway's most elaborate sketches. "We at length," he writes, "reached the top of the mountain ridge, and suddenly turning the point of a cliff that jutted out, and checked the road, we came abruptly into a hollow, something like a crater of an extinct volcano, which was filled almost entirely by a lovely lake, on the right hand side of which rose the highest peak of the mountain, composed of compact silicious sandstone—so bare, so white, so serrated, so tempest-worn, so vexed with all the tempests of the Atlantic, that if mere matter could suffer, we might suppose that this lofty and precipitous peak presented the portrait of material endurance ; and still, though white was the prevailing colour, yet not one tint or shadowing that decks and paints a mountain's brow was wanting. Here were the brown heath, the gray lichen, the green fern, the red crane's-bill; and straight down the cliff, from its topmost peak to the water's side, was branded in a dark and blasted line, the downward track of a meteoric stone that had fallen from the atmosphere, and, shattering itself against the mountain's crest, rolled down in fiery and smoking fragments into the adjacent lake. Last year, amidst the crash of a thunder-storm, this phenomenon occurred, and the well-defined line of its burning progress is and will be for years apparent. On the other side of the lake, a fair, verdant bank presented itself, courting the traveller to sit down and take his rest, after winding his toilsome way up the long ascent into this peaceful and unexpected retreat; gentle and grassy knolls were here and there interspersed, on which sheep, of most picturesque leanness, some black and some white, with primitive crumpled horns, were grazing. But the lake—not a breath was abroad on its expanse; it smiled as it reflected the gray mountain and the azure face of heaven; it seemed as if on this day the spirit of the Atlantic had fallen asleep, and air, earth, and ocean were celebrating the festival of repose; the waters of the lake, of the colour and clearness of the sky, were

'·Blue—darkly, deeply, beautifully blue.'

You could look down a hundred fathoms deep, and still no bottom; speckled trouts floating at immense depths, seemed as if they soared in ether. Then the stillness of the whole scene; you seemed lifted, as it were, out of the turmoil of the world into some planetary paradise, into some such place as the apostle, in the Apocalypse, was invited to, when the voice said, 'Come up hither.' You might have supposed that sound had no existence here, were it not that now and then a hawk shrieked while towering over the mountain top, or a lamb bleated beneath as it ran to its mother. I could have gone to sleep here, and dreamt of heaven, purchased for poor sinners like me by a Saviour's blood; I did, at any rate, praise the God of nature and of grace, and drew near to Him in Christ, grateful for all His blessings and all His wonders of creating and redeeming love. But the day was advancing; we had farther to go, and much to do, and my friend drew me away from my abstraction and repose, that had settled and softened into prayer. So we mounted our ponies and rode about a quarter of a mile along a level road, as smooth as a gravel-walk, that coasted the lake until we came to a steep bank, where we let our horses graze along the water's edge, and ascended a ridge or ruin, as I may call it, of the cup or crater, in which we were embosomed. All of a sudden the most magnificent prospect that ever met my eye presented itself—the whole range of the northern coast of Donegal. Seemingly beneath your feet, but really some miles off, lay the expanse of the Atlantic Ocean, like eternity, before you, over which fancy flew, and almost impelled you to strain your eyes to catch a glimpse of America. Some leagues out at sea, but apparently within your grasp, lay Torry Island, rising out of the deep like a castellated and fortified city ; lofty towers, church spires, battle-ments, bastions, batteries, presented themselves, so varied and so fantastically deceptive were its cliffs. . . . . Directly under us was a most curious picture to be seen ; the mountain on which we stood, as it descended to the west, presented sundry shelves or valleys, in each of which lay a round and beauteous lake. These tarns looked like mirrors set in the mountain's side to reflect the upright sun ; and five or six of such sheets of silver presented themselves, until at the very root of the mountain, a large expanse of water, a mile or two over, studded with islands, sufficiently wooded to be ornamental, finished the whole picture, and formed the last beauty and curiosity I shall record of this surpassingly interesting hill."*

From Kilmacrenan, the road traverses hilly ground, enlivened by views of the valley of the Lannan, as it flows down to Lough Fern, and the more distant Glennalla hills rising between Mulroy Bay and Lough Swilly. After a long and tedious hill, the traveller gets a splendid view over the valley of the Swilly, extending from the Gartan mountains on the right, away to the green slopes of the Laggan. The road now descends into a pleasant vale, and we enter

* Otway's Sketches in Donegal.

LETTERKENNY, (Hotel, Hegarty's,) a pleasant little town of one long street, occupying the side of a hill, and overlooking a large expanse of country. In the centre of the town is a clock-tower, and above it, on a hill, is the Protestant church, and hard by the Catholic cathedral, adjoining to which is a handsome convent. It was at Letterkenny that Theobald Wolfe Tone was taken prisoner in 1798, immediately after the defeat of the French squadron, by Sir J. B. Warren's fleet, off Torry Island. "The *Hoche*, in which Tone was embarked, during six hours maintained a most determined but unavailing struggle with four sail of the line and a frigate. Tone commanded one of the batteries, and during the engagement fought with the utmost desperation, and as if he was courting death! When the *Hoche* struck, and was taken into Lough Swilly, the prisoners were landed and marched to Letterkenny. The officers, amongst whom Tone passed for a Frenchman, were invited to breakfast at Lord Cavan's. One of the guests, (his son states,) a former friend and fellow-student in the University, Sir George Hill, recognised Tone, addressed him by name, and denounced him to Lord Cavan." * Letterkenny is a quarter sessions town, and has a very good weekly market. Its clean street,

* " The United Irishmen," R. R. Madden, vol. i., Third Series.

its range of gas-lamps, and other pleasant tokens of an improving spirit, bear honourable testimony to the efficiency of the town-commissioners and their excellent chairman, Joseph Gallaher, Esq.

I. Excursion to Gartan Lough.

The road passes through the beautiful grounds of Ballymacool, (J. Boyd, Esq.,) adjoining the town, and at the end of the first mile skirts the old churchyard of Conwall, where there was an ancient monastery important enough to give a name to the parish, and a village remarkable for its connexion with one of the most noteworthy incidents in the history of Tirconnell.   In the year 1257 was fought the famous battle of Creadran-Cillè in Northern Sligo, between Geoffrey or Godfrey O'Donnell, Lord of Tirconnell, and the renowned Maurice Fitzgerald, the then lord-deputy of Ireland. Both leaders met in a personal encounter.   O'Donnell gained the advantage, but he carried his death-wound from the combat.   About a year after, while he was still lying ill of his wounds on an island in the secluded Lough Beathath,* messengers came from O'Neil, demanding hostages and other tokens of submission.   O'Donnell's answer was to summon the Tirconnellians from all quarters to

* The present Lough Beath, or Veagh.

wait on him. " Having assembled at their lord's call, he ordered them, as he was not able to lead them, to prepare for him the coffin in which his remains should be buried, to place him therein, and to carry him in the very midst of his people. He told them to fight bravely, as he was amongst them, and not to fear the power of their enemies. They then proceeded in battle array, at the command of their lord, to meet O'Neil's force, till both armies confronted each other on the banks of the Swilly." *
After a hard-fought battle the Tyronians were routed, and the Tirconnellians, returning from the field, laid down the coffin in which Godfrey lay on the street of the village of Conwall, and the brave chieftain immediately expired.

"Now proud and high Tirconnell shouts, but bleeding on the gale
Upon the ear ascendeth now a sad and sullen wail;
For on that field, as back they bore, from chasing of the foe,
The spirit of O'Donnell fled!—Oh, woe for Ulster, woe!

"Yet died he there all gloriously—a victor in the fight—
A chieftain at his people's head, a warrior in his might.
They dug him there a fitting grave, upon that field of pride—
And a lofty cairn raised above, by fair Lough Swilly's side." †

No trace now remains either of the monastery or the village, except, perhaps, a portion of the walls of the old chapel. There is a legend that the village was utterly destroyed by a fire occasioned by cats, and that it was never afterwards rebuilt. On a

* Annals of the Four Masters, A.D. 1258.   † Ballad.

slope on the opposite side of the valley is Rockhill, (J. Stewart, Esq.)

Following up the right bank of the Swilly, the road passes the glebe-house, (Rev. Mr Kingsmil,) embosomed in a dark wood, under which is the historic Scariff-Hollis, a ford on the Swilly, which was, in former times, one of the chief passes into the hill country of Tirconnell. It was over this that the celebrated Shane O'Neil fled after his defeat, by Hugh Duv. O'Donnell, in 1567, and it was at this pass that Bishop Heber M'Mahon was driven to fight or surrender to the English, under Sir Charles Coote and Colonel Venables, on the 21st June 1650. Heber M'Mahon chose to fight, but the English cavalry, more than twice as numerous as his, all but annihilated his little army. The people of the locality say the place has been called Scariff-Hollis—*i. e.*, "the ford of the light," from the circumstance of the flashing of ordnance keeping up a light over the ford there during the night previous to the battle. Many a saddle was emptied of its rider on that day; and the horses, left to themselves, continued long after to roam about on the hill above, which has been since, from this circumstance, called Crock-na-neach—*i. e.*, "the hill of the horses." Two miles beyond Scariff-Hollis, the road leaves the bank of the Swilly, and ascends a rising ground, having Foxhall (G. Chambers, Esq.) on the right, crosses Drumbolog bridge about two miles farther on, and, passing Temple Douglas, where once stood an abbey, some remains of which are incorporated with the wall now enclosing the graveyard, in a lonely vale where Gay might have written his elegy, is carried up the side of the valley of the Lannan to Churchill, beyond which, at a short distance, is

GARTAN LOUGH, or Lough Beagh, South, which, with its wooded banks, breaks on the eye with peculiar pleasure. There are in reality two lakes at Gartan, separated by a very narrow neck of land, the upper being named Lough-a-gibbon, while the lower and larger one is Lough Gartan proper. *Trollius europeus* flourishes on these lakes. Bordering Gartan lake is the beautiful residence of J. Stewart, Esq., and on the strip of land between the two Loughs is a glebe-house, (Rev. Mr Maturin.) On the western side of the upper lake are the remains of a chapel and abbey, built on the spot where St Colum Cillè* was born in 521. "The father of the Culdees," says the Rev. C. Otway, "could not come to birth in a more appropriate place." An incident, touching in itself and illustrative of the

---

* Anglicised into Columkille. A notice of this saint, whose name occurs so often in the traditions, written and unwritten, of Tirconnell, is given in its proper place in the historic sketch at the beginning of this volume

saint's affection for his birthplace, is related by Adamnan, who "thought it so interesting that it ought to be mentioned." * On a certain occasion, while Columba was in Iona, he told one of the brothers that a crane, driven about by various winds, should come, weary and fatigued, and lie down on the beach of the island quite exhausted. "Treat that bird tenderly," said the saint ; "bring it to some neighbouring house, where it may be kindly received, and well nursed for three days and three nights. When the crane is refreshed after that time, unwilling to sojourn any longer in this strange land, it shall fly back directly to its lovely home in Ireland. I am very anxious about this bird, because it comes from my own native place." The good brother obeyed, for the bird came, and after three days of careful nursing, gently rose on its wings to a great height, and marking its path through the air homewards, it directed its course across the sea to Ireland, straight as it could fly on a calm day." The lake reposes at the base of Glendowan Mountains, which rise from its shore in an amphitheatre, enclosing it on the north and west. Otway describes it as "one of the finest of those numerous sheets of water which are interspersed through the valleys and mountains of this highland

* Adamnan's Life, Trans., p. 56.

district; either in the midst of the mountains, forming the sources of rivers, or in the lowland valleys expanding as their receptacles or reservoirs. High or low, small or large, they form interesting objects for the tourist; and I am not sure whether, in this way, our Irish lake may not be found as worthy of a visit, as one in Cumberland, or Scotland, or even Switzerland."* Running north-west from the upper lake is Derryveagh, the scene of the "Adair evictions," some sixty families having been turned out there on the hill side, and their roof-trees broken down in one day. The tourist may return by Kilmacrenan to Letterkenny.

II. EXCURSION TO RAPHOE.

Passing the port of Letterkenny, the traveller journeys down the valley of the Swilly for about a mile, and then turning to the right holds a south-east course over an uninteresting country to Raphoe, (8½ miles,) which is well placed at the foot of the great range of Donegal mountains, as they begin to decline unto the lowlands. Raphoe, anciently *Rath-Both*, "the rath of the cottages," is one of the oldest towns in Ireland. St Colum Cillè established a monastery here, which was subsequently enlarged or restored by St Adamnan, who

* Sketches in Donegal.

converted the place into a bishopric. St Eunan was
appointed the first bishop of this see, who so far
back as the eleventh century built the cathedral,
which, with some notable alterations, stands there
to this day. It is a plain cruciform building, with
a square tower of the last century, which is also
the date of the transepts added by Bishop Pooley
in 1702. The venerable diocess of Raphoe was
incorporated with that of Derry by Act of Parliament in 1835, and the episcopal residence now
stands near the cathedral in a ruinous condition.
The Catholic ecclesiastical division remains what it
has been from the earliest times, but the Catholic
bishop of the diocess resides at Letterkenny. The
town has declined much of late years; whole rows
of houses are in a state of dilapidation. There is a
fine example of a stone circle at Beltanny, on the
summit of a hill about two miles from the town.
This circle consists of sixty-seven stones, and
measures one hundred and fifty yards in circumference. The name Beltanny is supposed to be a
corruption of *Baal-tinne,* "the fire of Baal," inti-
mating a spot where that deity was particularly
worshipped in Ireland; and just the same is the
etymology in Gaelic for the Beltani tree, burned at
Midsummer.

The land around Raphoe, especially towards the

south and east, is fertile and highly cultivated; the surface of the country is hilly. Fine views may be got from Mullafin (954 feet) eastward, over the green undulations and valleys of the Deel and Fin, and beyond the Foyle away to the distant hills of county Derry, while on every other side the Donegal ranges darken the horizon. Close at hand, on the north-west, is Cark mountain, (1205 feet,) near the sum-mit of which, some ten miles from Raphoe, is Lough Deel, in which the Burndale, as it is com-monly called here, takes its rise. This stream flows a little south of Convoy and Raphoe, through Bal-lindrate, and joins the Foyle a little below Lifford.

From Raphoe the tourist may proceed through Ballindrate—a village with nothing to characterize it, except, perhaps, that the river is navigable by small craft up to this point—on to Lifford and Stra-bane. But there is more of incident on the road to Stranorlar, through Convoy, (three miles,) a village in which the traveller will find nothing to attract his notice except the Protestant and Catholic churches, facing each other across the road, and the well-wooded demesne of G. Montgomery, Esq. "Hard by, near Convoy," writes the Rev. C. Otway, "I observed a kind of magnesian stone or steatite, that might be applied to many uses in architecture and the arts; it is as easily cut and carved as a piece of wood ; it bears the fire so well that it would answer for crucibles."*

From Convoy the road traverses an open country, passing Tircallan, a residence belonging to the Marquis of Conyngham, and affording near views of the Donegal Highlands, to Stranorlar, where "the only building of interest is a very handsome Roman Catholic church, lately built" by the Rev. D. E. Coyle. In the neighbourhood are Drimboe Castle, (Sir S. Hayes ;) Summer Hill, (J. Johnston, Esq. ;) and Meenglass, (Viscount Lifford.) Stranorlar is the birthplace of Frances Browne, the well-known blind poetess of Donegal.

STRANORLAR TO DONEGAL.

Crossing the Finn, the road passes through Ballyboffey, a busy, thriving village, and following up the valley of the Burn Darnett, affords extensive views over the open country behind. A short distance above Ballyboffey, a road is given off to the left, which leads to Meenglass, (the green-plane,) the seat of Viscount Lifford, a nobleman whose large intellect can find interesting occupation amongst his tenantry in the remote Donegal. At the sixth mile Lough Mourne is reached, and the tourist, now fairly in the highland country, follows

* Sketches in Donegal.

the road already sketched in an excursion from Donegal to the Gap of Barnesmore.

FROM STRANORLAR TO GLENTIES.

Some very pretty scenery is to be met with by following the Finn up its stream on the north bank to Fintown, or on the south bank to Glenties. Emerging from Ballyboffey, the road runs alongside the river, on the opposite bank of which are the dense woods of Drumboe Castle, and passing Glenmore, (W. M. Style, Esq.,) four miles farther on, cuts round the base of Altnapaste, a conical hill, (1199 feet,) which on this side comes close to the river's brink. If it be dry weather, the traveller will not fail to notice the marked attrition of this mountain stream, which has furrowed deeply the solid rock that forms its bed. On the northern bank, opposite to Altnapaste, are a Catholic chapel, and a little higher up the valley, a Protestant chapel and glebe-house, backed up by Crocknamona. Here a road is given off to the right, which, crossing the Finn, "where there is a pretty waterfall," and falling into the road on the northern bank at Cloghan Lodge, (Sir T. C. Style,) keeps along the river to its source at Fintown, some ten miles up in the heart of the mountains.

o

The direct road leads on to Glenties, and affords along its whole length highland scenery, rich and varied as the tourist could desire. Crossing the Reelan bridge, we find ourselves in the midst of the mountains. As we follow up the Reelan river, we get at every turn of the road new views of a noble group of steeply-escarped hills, which "shoulder each other" close on the left. First is Gaugin, (1865 feet,) conspicuous by its dark colour and isolated summit; then Crovenahanta, (1568 feet,) and Lavaghmore, (2211 feet,) and Croaghanairigid, (Silver Hill,) and other peaks of the Croaghgorm, or Bluestack, range peering up behind. On the right is Crocknahamid, up whose side we have been ascending; and a little farther on, Boultypatrick, (1415 feet.) Having reached the watershed at a point eight hundred feet above the level of the sea, the road begins to descend Ballinagrath Hill, affording fine views northward over Aghla, Scraigs, and the Glendowan mountains. A little farther on we pass Lough Ea, a small tarn guarded by savage-looking precipices, under an outlier of the Binbane range, which the eye may trace from this point westward behind Ardara, and running out to the ocean cliffs of Slievatoovey. From Lough Ea, our road is down the rapidly-descending course of the Owen-Ea, into the Glenmore, or Glen of Glenties, one of the most beautiful of Highland valleys. The gray mountain peaks, standing in threatening line at the head of the glen, the brown hills subsiding into green slopes, the meadowy holms, over which the stream wanders, recalling by its many windings the poet's beautiful fancy of the river unwilling to leave its source, all realize Dante's idea of the *dolcemente feroce.* * From Martin's Bridge the valley lies smiling before you into Glenties.

LETTERKENNY TO RATHMULLAN.

It is a pleasant drive on the western side of the Swilly, passing Gortlee, Kiltoy Lodge, Lisnennan Lodge, on the left, and on the right Barn Hill, Castle Wray, and Castle Grove, at which point (four miles) the direct road turns inland; but the tourist had better follow that which keeps to the right, for the sake of the beautiful views of Lough Swilly and its coasts. Beyond Ardrumman House (F. Mansfield, Esq.) are the ruins of Killydonnell Abbey, a Franciscan monastery, founded in the six-teenth century by an O'Donnell, and a chapel of ease to the ecclesiastical establishment of Kilmacrenan. A large portion of the side-walls of the chapel still remain, and a turret or gable, from which the

* Sweetly fierce.

visitor may have a view of one of the most beautiful landscapes on earth.   Below him is a land-locked sea of purest sapphire, bordered by a coast, green to the water's edge, and, dotted with waving woods and handsome residences, slopes pleasantly off to the hills of Fanad and Inishowen.

> "The bowery shore
> Went off in gentle windings to the hoar
> And light blue mountains, but no breathing man
> With a warm heart, and eye prepared to scan
> Nature's clear beauty, could pass lightly by
> Objects that looked out so invitingly
> On either side.   .   .   .
> The sidelong view of swelling leafiness,
> Which the glad setting sun in gold doth dress,
> Whence ever and anon the joy outsprings,
> And seals upon the beauty of its wings.
> The lovely turret shattered and outworn,
> Stands venerably proud : too proud to mourn
> Its long-lost grandeur." *

The bell of the Abbey of Killydonnell, according to a pretty legend, is heard once every seven years at midnight.   The story goes that a party of marauders from Tyrone attacked the abbey, and carrying off amongst other things the bell, put it on board a vessel which they had waiting off the shore below, and departed with their booty across the lough.   But God's justice overtook them, for a storm arose, and the sacrilegious robbers were all

* Keats.

drowned, and thus the sacred bell never entered Tyrone. It is kept somewhere at the bottom of the lough, whence its muffled tones proceed once every seven years at the still hour of midnight.

Beyond the Abbey of Killydonnell is the demesne of Fort Stewart, (Sir James Stewart, Bart.,) which occupies a beautiful situation close to the shore, where there is a ferry of the same name, touching on the opposite side at a point within about eight miles of Derry. At a short distance farther on are Shellfield, (N. Stewart, Esq.,) and the ruins of old Fort Stewart, a place built at the commencement of the seventeenth century. From hence the road traverses a well-cultivated country to

RATHMELTON, which is prettily situated on the Lannan, a picturesque mountain stream that flows by Kilmacrenan into Lough Fern, emerging from it under the same name, only a few yards from its point of entrance. Like the Bann, it was at one time famous for its pearls. There is good salmon and trout fishing on this river. Leave to fish must be obtained from Sir James Stewart, the owner of the river, or from Mr Charles Kelly, Rathmelton, who rents it.

Distances.—Millford, 4 miles; Kilmacrenan, 6½ miles; Rathmullan, 6½ miles; Fort Stewart Ferry, 3; Killydonnell, 4.

Rathmelton is a good starting-point for an excursion to Kilmacrenan and Gartan Lough, (p. 200.)

The road running from Rathmelton to Milford cuts off the peninsula formed by Lough Swilly and Mulroy Bay : it is only five miles from sea to sea. Leaving Rathmelton, the tourist may take the direct road to Milford, or go round by Tilly bridge, by which route he will get an abundance of interesting scenery along the picturesque valley of the Lannan, by the pretty seats of Claragh, (Mrs Watt,) and Ballyarr, (Lord George Hill,) and Lough Fern, which is a sheet of water about four miles in circumference, and the centre of a landscape exquisitely beautiful.

There is much besides Lough Fern in the neighbourhood of Milford to interest the lover of scenery. The visitor should not fail to explore the Bunlin river, a stream which pursues a romantic course all the way down to the Mulroy Bay, forming a fine cascade at the Golden Loup.

The Mulroy is an estuary which for irregularity of coast-line is hardly equalled anywhere. To explore this extraordinary inlet of the Atlantic, so full of various incident, the tourist should go from Milford to Carrigart by the road that keeps along the western shore of the bay, of whose calm waters and bold and broken shores it affords beautiful views. Carrigart is a small village, with nothing to detain the tourist; but in its neighbourhood are the Rosapenna sands[*] and Downing's Bay, from above which there is a glorious view of Sheephaven,[†] and its magnificent background of mountains. Close on the left, rises Lough Salt mountain,[‡] at the foot of which repose the village of Glen, and the lough of the same name.

From Carrigart the tourist should again seek the Mulroy shore by the nearest route, and crossing the ferry from Lowertown, follow the road on the eastern side, traversing Fanad,[§] the land of the famous Gallowglasses, " the MacSweenys of the axes." Fanad was " the property of 'the sept of the O'Breslans, descendants of Connaing, third son of Conaill Gulban, son of Niall of the Nine Hostages, who possessed Tirconnell.' The O'Breslans, however, were succeeded by the MacSwynes, who established themselves and built several fortresses. Physically speaking, Fanet is intersected by three short ranges of hills running across the peninsula, viz., the Rathmullan range, . . . the Knockalla Hills, which attain to a height of 1200 feet; and a still more northerly group about 800 feet."[||]

The road skirting the base of the Knockalla Hills,

---

[*] See p. 190.   [†] Page 189.   [‡] Page 195.
[§] Written Fanad, Fanet, Fanait.   [||] Murray.

and keeping close to the shore, abounds in all the incident of exciting coast scenery, and affords fine views of mountain ranges away to the left. About a mile or so from Rosnakil, on one of the inlets of the Mulroy, is the tower of Moross Castle, one of the many fortresses belonging to the MacSwynes. The pedestrian, who is fond of cliff scenery, should proceed northwards by one of the pathways over the mountains, to explore the cliffs at Rinmore Point, and continue on to the lighthouse, (ninety feet above high water,) on Fanet Head, and return southward by the coast of Lough Swilly to Rathmullan. The distance from Fanet Head to Dunaff, on the opposite side of the entrance into Lough Swilly, is only four miles.

There is a car-road running from Rosnakil across the peninsula between the Knockalla Hills, and appearing on Lough Swilly over Ballymacstocker Bay, where the *Saldanha* was wrecked in 1811, and from thence along the coast to Doagh, one of the most primitive native villages that it is possible to conceive. The coast scenery here is particularly fine, especially at the Seven Arches, a series of marine caves accessible by land. Near the Brown George Rock is a splendid natural arch, (eighty feet in height.)

As the tourist proceeds southward, along the

coast, passing the Knockalla Battery, he gets fine views over Lough Swilly and the Inishowen seaboard, and the mountains in the background culminating in Slieve Snaght. Looking up the Lough one gets a lovely view of quiet water and woody shore, while close on the right are the Knockalla Hills, whose broken summit-line and numerous offshoots give grandeur and variety to the soft beauty of the landscape. Near Lamb's Head Bay, at a village called Drumhallagh, is a tolerably perfect Giant's Bed, formed of large flat stones placed on their edge. Leaving Lamb's Head Bay behind, your road descends into a pretty country skirting Kinnegar strand, and, passing the glebe-house, Drumhallagh House, Fort Royal, and Rathmullan House, (the beautiful residence of T. Batt, Esq.,) you enter

RATHMULLAN, a little town charmingly situated on the very edge of Lough Swilly's pleasant shore. Behind is a range of hills, the highest point of which, Crockanaffrin, is 1137 feet. It is worth while to make an excursion to the top of this hill or Croaghan, (1010 feet,) which is nearer; for the extraordinary view over the inlets and indentations of this singular coast will put the traveller more in mind of Norwegian fiords than British scenery. In the town are the ruins of a Carmelite priory, "and a castle adjoining, formerly occupied by the M'Swine

Faugh, the possessor of Fanait. The eastern part, used as a church until a late period, exhibits considerable traces of pointed Gothic architecture. Over the east window there still remains a figure of St Patrick. The architecture of the remainder of the building is of the Elizabethan age, a great part of it having been rebuilt by Bishop Knox, of the diocess of Raphoe, in 1618, on obtaining possession of the manor of Rathmullan from Turlogh Oge M'Swine."[*]

Rathmullan is characterized by two of the most deeply interesting incidents in the history of Tirconnell. Towards the end of the sixteenth century there was growing up in Tirconnell, a youth, "whose name and renown spread through the five provinces of Ireland, even before he had arrived at the age of manhood, for his goodly growth, wisdom, sagacity, and noble deeds, and the people in general used to say that he was really the prophesied one."[†] This was Hugh Roe, heir-presumptive to the throne of Tirconnell, his father, then an old man, being the reigning chieftain. Sir John Perrott, the then lord-deputy of Ireland, determined to get possession of the young prince, and with this view had a ship fitted up and well stored with Spanish wines. The vessel sailed round from Dublin, and put into Lough Swilly, in which neighbourhood the young

---

[*] Lord George Hill.   [†] Annals of the Four Masters, A.D. 1587.

O'Donnell was staying with his foster-father, Mac-Swyne-na-Thua ;* and the crew, representing themselves as Spanish traders, opened a traffic in wines with the people on the shore. The scheme succeeded. Hugh Roe and some young companions, coming into the neighbourhood of Rathmullan, were invited by MacSwyne of Fanad, the lord of the castle at Rathmullan, to an entertainment in which they should try the quality of the wine newly imported. A messenger was sent from the castle for a good supply, but word was sent back by the captain that all the wine they had for sale had been disposed of ; if, however, the noble company at the castle would condescend to visit the ship, he should take it as a great honour to treat them to the choicest samples in his stock. There was no need to press the warm invitation.

> " The generous prince, Red Hugh,
> Unguarded quits the fortress walls and stands amidst the crew ;
> Down with the hatches, set the sails, we've won the wished-for
>   prize ;
> Above the rebel's prison-cell to-morrow's sun shall rise.
> Untasted foams the Spanish wine, the board is spread in vain ;
> The hand that waved a welcome forth is shackled by a chain ;
> Yet faster, faster through the deep, the vessel glideth on—
> Tirconnell's towers like phantoms fade, the last faint trace is
>   gone."†

---

* The MacSwyne of the Axes.   † Ballad.

The reader will find the subsequent career of Hugh Roe briefly sketched in the historical notice of Tirconnell, prefixed to these excursions.

The little town of Rathmullan witnessed another incident far more important and far more touching than the kidnapping of the young Hugh Roe. This event is known as "the flight of the Earls." A ship carried from Rathmullan "the Earl O'Neil, (Hugh, son of Ferdoragh,) and the Earl O'Donnell, (Rory, son of Hugh, who was son of Manus,) and many other nobles of the province of Ulster. These are the persons who went with O'Neil, namely, his Countess Catherina, daughter of Magennis, and her three sons—Hugh the Baron, John, and Brian. . . . These were they who went with the Earl O'Donnell, namely, Caffar, his brother, with his sister, Nuala ; Hugh, the earl's child, wanting three weeks of being one year old ; Rose, daughter of O'Doherty, and wife of Caffar. . . . They embarked on the festival of the Holy Cross, in autumn, (1607.) This was a distinguished company ; and it is certain that the sea has not borne and the wind has not wafted, in modern times, a number of persons in one ship more eminent, illustrious, or noble in point of genealogy, heroic deeds, valour, feats of arms, and brave achievements than they. Would that God had but permitted them to remain in their patrimonial inheritances until their children should arrive at the age of manhood! Woe to the heart that meditated, woe to the mind that conceived, woe to the counsel that recommended the project of this expedition, without knowing whether they should to the end of their lives be able to return to their native principalities or patrimonies!"* "Davis concludes his curious narrative with a few pregnant words, in which the difficulties England had to contend with in conquering Tyrone, (Earl O'Neil,) are there acknowledged with all the frankness of a generous foe: 'As for us that are here,' he says, 'we are glad to see the day wherein the countenance and majesty of the law and civil government hath banished Tyrone out of Ireland, which the best army in Europe, and the expense of two millions of sterling pounds, had not been able to bring to pass.'"† Amongst Mangan's translations from the Irish is a touching elegy, said to have been composed by O'Donnell's own bard, Owen Roe MacWard, who accompanied the chieftain in his exile. This beautiful poem is addressed to Nuala, O'Donnell's sister, whom the bard finds in solitary grief at the grave of her illustrious relatives, on St Peter's Hill, at Rome.

* Annals of the Four Masters, A.D. 1607.
† Moore's Ireland.

" O woman of the piercing wail,
 Who mournest o'er yon mound of clay
  With sigh and groan,
Would to God thou wert among the Gael!
Thou wouldst not then from day to day
  Weep thus alone.

'Twere long before, around a grave
In green Tirconnell one could find
  This loneliness;
Near where Beann-Boirche's banners wave
Such grief as thine could ne'er have pined
  Companionless.

 . . . . . .

What do I say? Ah, woe is me!
Already we bewail in vain
  Their fatal fall!

 . . . . . .

Then, daughter of O'Donnell, dry
Thine overflowing eyes, and turn
  Thy heart aside,
For Adam's race is born to die,
And sternly the sepulchral urn
  Mocks human pride!

Look not, nor sigh, for earthly throne,
Nor place thy trust in arm of clay—
  But on thy knees
Uplift thy soul to God alone,
For all things go their destined way
  As He decrees.

Embrace the faithful Crucifix,
And seek the path of pain and prayer
  Thy Saviour trod;
Nor let thy spirit intermix
With earthly hope and worldly care
  Its groans to God!

And Thou, O mighty Lord! whose ways
Are far above our feeble minds
    To understand,
Sustain us in these doleful days,
And render light the chain that binds
    Our fallen land!

Look down upon our dreary state,
And through the ages that may still
    Roll sadly on,
Watch Thou o'er hapless Erin's fate,
And shield at least from darker ill
    The blood of Conn!"

From Rathmullan the tourist may cross, by boat, to Buncranna, on the east side of Lough Swilly, or proceed by the road to Rathmelton, which is a beautiful drive, passing the woods of Holymount, and Raywood. After crossing the Genalla river, where you get charming glimpses of the grounds of Glenalla House, and the pretty little church, built by General Hart, at Aughnish, you keep close to the shore up to Rathmelton.

FROM RATHMELTON TO BUNCRANA.

Lough Swilly is crossed from Fort-Stewart. The tourist will take the straight road to Newtowncunningham, a quiet hamlet, where there is nothing to detain him. Here, instead of going on to Derry, he should turn to the left, taking the Burt road, which runs northward, passing, about a mile and a half farther on, a place called Bridgetown,

near which are the remains of an old castle, on
Castle Hill. Close to Burt is the Greenan Hill,
(800 feet,) on the summit of which are the remains of the historic Grianan of Aileach,* the chief
residence in former times of the northern Hy Nial.

No man who knows anything of ancient Ireland
will omit a visit to this spot. As the word Grianan
signifies a *sunny chamber*, some have fancied that
there was at one time here some kind of temple or
place dedicated to the worship of the sun; but this
opinion seems to have no other foundation than the
etymology of the word. It is certain that it was
the principal *palace* of the northern Irish kings
from the earliest times down to the twelfth century.
It is a Cyclopean construction, consisting of a cashel,
whose circular wall encloses an area seventy-seven
feet in diameter. The wall is not vertical, but rises
with a curved incline, like that of Staigue Fort in
the county of Kerry. Within the thickness of the
wall are galleries beginning on either side of the
entrance, but strongly walled off from the gateway,
and running round one-half the entire circumference; they are entered from the area inside. In the
centre of the cashel is a small oblong building,
which, it is probable, was a chapel, and a more re-

* See the historic sketch *passim:* sometimes written " Oileach"
and " Ailigh."

cent erection than any other portion of the remains. Outside, the cashel is defended by three extensive ramparts, running in concentric circles. They are constructed of earth mixed with lines of uncemented stones. The hill on which the Grianan of Aileach stood is 800 feet above the sea, and would deserve a visit for the fine and varied prospect it affords. It commands the whole of the district called the Laggan. From this point the visitor may behold again the blue pomp of Lough Swilly, and the pageantry of its shores already traced from the venerable Killydonnell, on the opposite shore. Southward, the view extends far over the green slopes of the Laggan. Here is the traditionary Magh Ith,* the plain whereon was fought the first battle in Ireland. Here Ith, the son of Breogan, the first of the Milesians that landed in Ireland, received his death-wound.

"One of the most familiar legends of Inishowen is, that a troop of Hugh O'Neill's horse lies in magic sleep in a cave under the hill of Aileach, where the princes of the country were formerly installed. These bold troopers only wait to have the spell removed to rush to the aid of their country ; and a man (says the legend) who wandered accidentally into the cave, found them lying beside their horses,

---

* The *Magh Ith* (plain of Ith) has not been identified.

P

fully armed, and holding the bridles in their hands. One of them lifted his head, and asked, 'Is the time come?' and when he received no answer—for the intruder was too much frightened to reply—dropped back into his lethargy. Some of the old folk consider the story an allegory, and interpret it as they desire." This legend has inspired a beautiful ballad on Inishowen.

> " God bless the gray mountains of dark Donegal !
> God bless royal Aileach, the pride of them all ;
> For she sits evermore like a queen on her throne,
> And smiles on the valleys of green Inishowen.
> > And fair are the valleys of green Inishowen,
> > And hardy the fishers that call them their own—
> > A race that nor traitor nor coward have known,
> > Enjoy the fair valleys of green Inishowen."*

From Burt the tourist should proceed northward to visit the Inishowen district. Inishowen is the peninsula of Eoghan,† one of the sons of the famous Niall of the Nine Hostages, and founder of Kinel Owen, or the O'Neil family, who possessed it down to the fifteenth century, from which time the O'Dohertys, descendants of Conail Gulban, were lords of the district till the death of Sir Cahir O'Doherty in 1610. Leaving Burt, the road keeps along the shore of Lough Swilly, in view of the large island of Inch, passes Glebe House, Glen Col-

---

* Hon. C. G. Duffy.   † Pronounced " Owen."

lan, Fahan House, and crossing the beautiful valley of Fahan, often mentioned in the ecclesiastical records of Ireland, enters

BUNCRANA, (Hotel, Commercial,) "a pleasant and pretty little bathing-place, situated on the shores of Lough Swilly, between the embouchures of two rivers, the Mill and Crana."* Buncrana is a capital head-quarters from whence to explore the bold headlands at the entrance into Lough Swilly. Here, also, there is good sport for the angler. It has a harbour in which the imperial fleet might ride, but no trade, unless what is done in one mill for flax-spinning. It is the chief of the artillery stations guarding Loughs Swilly and Foyle, and one of the quarter-sessions towns of the county. "It was a place of comparative importance in the time of Elizabeth, but after the confiscation of Ulster, fell into great decay, but was restored and laid out in its present form by Sir John Vaughan, in 1717."† Near the present town was a castle of the O'Dohertys, which "is now incorporated with a modern building, and, with its approaches and gardens, is a picturesque object."‡ The visitor will get fine views from the summit of Meenkeeragh Hill, or the top of Mouldy Mountain, both of which are in the neighbourhood.

* Murray.   † Lewis's Topog. Dict.   ‡ Murray.

EXCURSION TO DUNREE HEAD.

Keeping along the base of Aghaweel Hill, (1106 feet,) pretty near the shore, and passing Linsfort and the ruin of Ross Castle, at Castleross bridge, the road (at the seventh mile) runs out to Dunree Head, (329 feet,) where there is a fort commanding the entrance into Lough Swilly. It will repay the pedestrian to proceed along the coast to Dunaff Head, (682 feet,) a noble headland defending Lough Swilly from the Atlantic. There is fine coast scenery all the way, with the Urris Hills close on the right; but the Gap of Mamore and the view from the top of Raghten-More, (1656 feet,) will especially interest him. From Dunaff Head the coast trends to the east, and affords abundance of exciting scenery along the shores of the Doagh and Trawbreaga Bays, which last runs up to within three miles of Carndonagh.

BUNCRAUNA TO MOVILLE.

Leaving Buncrana, the road turns inland, keeping along the left bank of the Owen-Crana for some three miles, after which it runs into the heart of the mountains, holding its way by Mintiagh's Lough, with Slieve Snaght, (2019 feet,) (which is not to be confounded with the mountain of the same name above Lough Barra,*) and the Urris Hills on the left, and at the end of the twelfth mile reaches

CARNDONAGH, "a neat little town, which chiefly supplies the commissariat of the Inishowen district. There is, however, but little to see here save a fine cross in the churchyard." †   From Carndonagh the tourist should proceed to Malin, a village situated at the head of Trawbreaga Bay, in which is Doagh island, having out at its north-western extremity the remains of Carrickabrahy Castle, one of the O'Doherty's fortalices.   The lover of cliff scenery should explore the coast from Malin on to Malin Head, eight and a half miles from the village, keeping along the cliffs from the Five Fingers to the Head, where there is a lighthouse and a coast-guard station.   From Malin Tower, which stands 226 feet over the waves, the cliffs trend to the south-east, forming a line of grand mural precipices, running some eight miles to Glengad Head.   "The cliffs are very magnificent, being upwards of 800 feet in height, and resembling those of Moher in County Clare, though not presenting the same sheer wall of precipice." ‡   From Glengad Head the pedestrian had better return to Malin.

Leaving Malin, after travelling about four miles

* Page 163.   † Murray.   ‡ Ibid.

of a good road, the tourist will cross the peninsula to Culdaff, where a river of the same name, a stream rising a few miles off in the mountains to the south, joins the sea.

> " See the bountiful Culdah,* careering along—
> A type of their manhood so stately and strong—
> On the weary for ever its tide is bestown,
> So they share with the stranger in fair Inishowen." †

From Culdaff, the road traverses for some miles a wild but not uninteresting district.   After the sixth mile or so it enters into a broad valley, with Squire's Cairn on the right, and Craignamaddy on the left, from which it emerges upon Lough Foyle, reaching at nine and a half miles

MOVILLE, (Hotel, Commercial,) "a watering-place which the citizens of Derry love to frequent in the summer," ‡ and it were hard to find a more lovely sea-side resort.   It is situated near the entrance to the Lough, so that all the shipping of Derry, which is an active port, passes under the windows.   Northward, the blue Atlantic bounds the horizon; while eastward there is a fine view extending from the coast away to the County Derry mountains, showing a fine range behind Newton-Limavaddy.   Immediately beyond Moville are the Squire's Cairn to the south-west, and Craignamaddy to the

* Culdaff.   † Ballad—C. G. Duffy.   ‡ Murray.

north-east, from both of which good views may be gained.

EXCURSION TO INISHOWEN HEAD.

It is a fine drive along the coast, passing Greencastle, where there is a good modern fort guarding the entrance into the Lough, between the Head and M'Gilligan Point opposite. Here also are the ruins of a fine old fortress belonging to the O'Dohertys, and three miles farther on Inishowen Head is reached, from which the lover of stern coast-scenery may set off on a most enjoyable scramble over the precipices that here face the Atlantic.

MOVILLE TO DERRY.

In the summer months the tourist may go from Moville to Derry by steamer, and a pleasanter trip than this it is not easy to find. About half-way up, the Lough expands into a splendid bay, narrowing again to an estuary at the famous Culmore, some four miles from Derry. It were hard to conceive a more beautiful landscape than that which greets one's eye as he passes up the river. Before him rises the " Maiden City," an amphitheatre of houses surmounted by the cathedral spire, and flanked on either side by green hills dotted with handsome residences. The highly-cultivated shores rise fresh and luxuriant from the calm water, going off gently to the peaceful hills of Inishowen on the right, and on the left to the blue forms of the more distant mountains of the County Derry. Should the tourist wish to go by the road, it is a charming drive of about nineteen miles to Derry. The road skirts the shore almost the whole way, affording beautiful views over the Foyle. The name of the Lough is said to be derived from Febhal, or Feval, a distinguished chief of the Tuath-de-Dannans. At the end of the eighth mile, you come to the small village of Carrowkeel, off which point the Foyle attains its greatest breadth. Having Crockglass (1296 feet) close upon the right, and crossing the Cabry stream, the road holds its course by the coast, passing, some four miles farther on, Eskaheen, the place where the renowned Eoghan, the first lord of Inishowen, was buried, though the exact site of the grave has not been determined. It was in this neighbourhood also that Toland, the teacher of Bolingbroke and leader of the English Deistical school in the reign of Queen Anne, was born. At a short distance from Eskaheen the traveller reaches Muff, a small village, adjoining which is Kilderry, (G. Hart, Esq.,) and down at the water's edge is the historic Fort of Culmore. Beyond

Culmore the road lies through a pleasant suburb into Derry. In the grounds of Belmont, about a mile from the city, is St Columb's stone—a mass of gneiss—which was long one of the inauguration stones of the chiefs of the district.

DERRY TO LETTERKENNY.

The direct road keeps along the right bank of the Foyle for the first two or three miles, and then bends westward to Newtowncunningham,* and from 'hence keeps along the Swilly sea-board, though the Lough does not appear till you approach Manorcunningham, a small village about fourteen miles from Derry, which the traveller will not be sorry to leave behind, to follow up the beautiful valley of the Swilly to Letterkenny. But for the general tourist the best route to Letterkenny is to go by railway to Burt, and thence by steamer on Lough Swilly, which plies during the summer months between that place and a point some two miles from Letterkenny, where he joins the main route.

DERRY TO STRANORLAR.

The tourist may go by rail to Stranorlar. Leaving the railway station at Derry, the line runs close

* Page 223.

to the beautiful estuary of the Foyle, passing Car-
rigans (four miles,) and St Johnstown (eight miles,)
which is now a miserable village, though, before the
Union, a borough returning a member to the Irish
Parliament.   Quitting St Johnstown, we pass, on
the right, a pretty Catholic church, built by Rev.
J. Stephens, and "a square tower, all that is left of
the Castle of Mountgevlin, in which James II. held
his court till the termination of the siege of Derry,"*
and pursue our way along the stately stream, crossing it above Porthall, (J. Clarke, Esq.,) thus passing
into Tyrone, in which county is Strabane, where we
now arrive.   A short mile from Strabane is Lifford,
the assize town of the County Donegal.   It may
be easily understood how Lifford, situated at an important military position at the confluence of the Finn
and the Mourne, which here unite their waters to
form the Foyle, which flows in a majestic stream
from hence to Derry, was one of the hardest and
oftenest contested points on the frontiers of Tirconnell.   It was while staying in his castle here, built to
resist the encroachments of the O'Neils, that Manus
O'Donnell composed his Irish Life of St Colum Cillè,
the kinsman and patron saint of his family.   In
the year 1600, Nial Garv O'Donnell having joined
the English, established himself in the Castle of

* Murray.

Lifford, and held it against the celebrated Hugh Roe O'Donnell. *

From Strabane the train carries the traveller on the Finn Valley Railway along the bank of the river Finn, passing Castlefin, where once stood a castle from which the O'Donnells ruled the district down to the beginning of the seventeenth century, and Killygordan, a clean village, a little higher up, and comes to a full stop at Stranorlar.

STRABANE TO LETTERKENNY.

The majority of travellers in Donegal enter the county by the road from Strabane to Letterkenny. This road (fifteen and a half miles) is carried over hilly ground, affording nothing special to interest the general tourist, unless indeed he be concerned in the flax crop ; this is a flax country, *par excellence*, as the traveller will be sure to perceive if he happen to pass this way in the end of August, or the beginning of September, during which season the air is impregnated with the abominable odour of that fibrous plant. There are good views from some points of the route over the valley of Foyle and the valley of the Swilly, into which the road falls at the tenth mile, and pursues its way up to Letterkenny.

* Page 37.

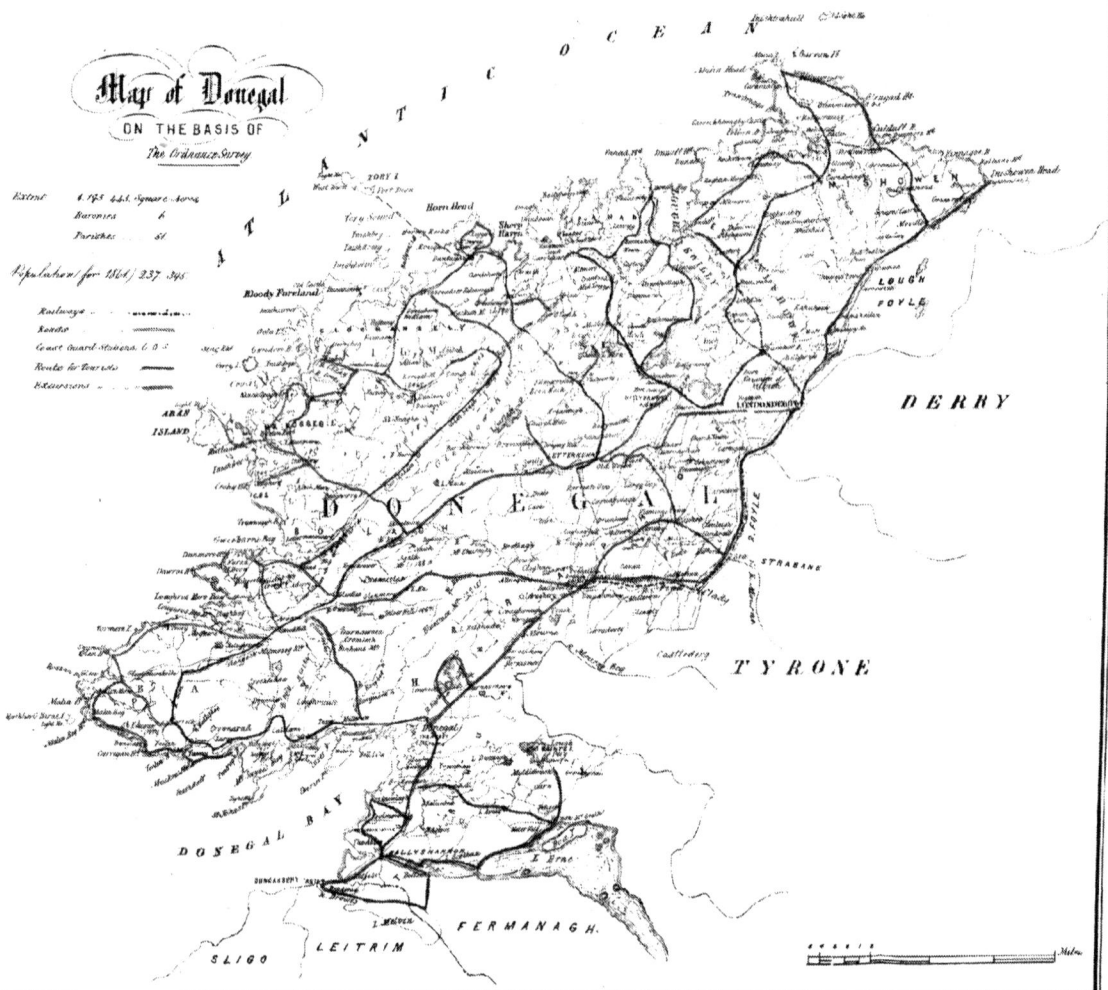

Map of Donegal

ON THE BASIS OF

The Ordnance Survey

Extent . . . 4,193,443 Square Acres

Baronies . . . 6

Parishes . . . 51

Population for 1861 237,395

Railways . . . .
Roads . . . .
Coast Guard Stations . C.G.S.
Routes for Tourists . . . .
Excursions . . . .

ATLANTIC OCEAN

DERRY

TYRONE

DONEGAL BAY

SLIGO   LEITRIM   FERMANAGH.

DONEGAL

Miles

ROUTES FOR TOURISTS IN DONEGAL.

[Ballyshannon is the best starting-point for a tour of Donegal. The traveller may get here either from Enniskillen or from Sligo.]

I.

THREE WEEKS IN DONEGAL.

1st Day, Ballyshannon—Excursion to Bundoran—Kinlough—Lough Melvin—Garrison.

2d, Ballyshannon to Kilbarron *Castle*—Coolmore—Ballintra—The Pullens, at Brownhall—Donegal.

3d, Excursion to Lough Esk and Barnesmore—Go on to Killybegs in the afternoon.

4th, Killybegs—The Caves of Muckross Point—Kilcar—Carrick—Slieve League.
  Return to Carrick.

5th, Car to Glen—Walk, or ride on horseback to Glen Head and the Sturrall—Walk to Tormore, Slieveatooey, Maghery, Ardara—Car to Glengesh in the evening.
    The non-pedestrian will go by the car-road from Carrick by Glengesh and Ardara.

6th, Ardara—Kilclooney Cromlech—Portnoo—Naran—Portachury—Glenties—The Glens.

7*th*, Glenties (start early)—Lough Finn—Ducarry—Lough Barra—Lough Beagh (or Veagh)—Dunlewy Lough—Gweedore Hotel.

8*th*, Excursion to Errigal—Dungloe—Crohy Head—Sleep at Dungloe.

9*th*, Dungloe—Burtonport—Islands of Rutland and Arran (north)—Get on to Gweedore Hotel.

10*th*, Gweedore Hotel—Falcarragh—Dunfanaghy—Excursion to Horn Head, and, weather permitting, to Torry Island.

11*th*, Dunfanaghy—Creslough—Kilmacrenan—Lough Salt—Letterkenny.

12*th*, Excursion from Letterkenny to Raphoe—Lifford—Return to Letterkenny.

13*th*, Letterkenny—Gartan Lough (by the Swilly)—Kilmacrenan (passing near the Rock of Doon)—Lough Fern—Rathmelton.

14*th*, Rathmelton (start early)—Milford—Carrigart—Cross Mulroy Bay by ferry-boat—Rathmullan.

15*th*, Rathmullan—Excursion to Fanad Head (see the Seven Arches)—Climb Croaghin Hill—Rathmelton.

16*th*, Rathmelton—Fort Stewart Ferry—Burt—Grianan of Aileach—Buncrana.

17*th*, Buncrana—Clonmany—Carndonagh—Malin—Excursion to Malin Head.

18*th*, Malin—Culdaff—Moville—Derry.

II.

TEN DAYS IN DONEGAL.

1*st Day*, Ballyshannon—Ballintra (see the Pullens)—Donegal—Excursion to Lough Esk and Barnesmore—Get on to Killybegs.

2*d*, Killybegs—Carrick—Slieve League.

3*d*, Carrick—Glen (Slieveatooey)—Glengesh—Ardara—Glenties.

4*th*, Glenties—Ducarry—Lough Barra—Lough Beagh (Veagh)—Dunlewy Lough—Gweedore.

5*th*, Excursion to Errigal—Falcarragh—Dunfanaghy.

6*th*, Dunfanaghy (see Horn Head)—Kilmacrenan—Letterkenny.

8*th*, Letterkenny—Rathmelton—Milford—Mulroy Bay—Cross Fanad to Rathmullen—Back to Rathmelton.

9*th*, Rathmelton—Fort-Stewart Ferry—Burt (see Aileach)—Buncrana—Clonmany—Malin.

10*th*, Excursion to Malin-Head—Culdaff—Moville—Derry.

III.

A WEEK IN DONEGAL.

1st Day, Ballyshannon—Donegal—Excursion to Lough Esk and Barnesmore—Killybegs.

2d, Killybegs—Carrick—Excursion to Slieve League—Glengesh—Ardara.

3d, Ardara (start early)—Glenties—Ducarry—Glenveagh—Gweedore.

4th, Gweedore Hotel—Dunfanaghy—Kilmacrenan—Letterkenny.

5th, Letterkenny—Rathmelton—Rathmullan—Cross the Ferry to Buncrana.

6th, Buncrana—Carndonagh—Moville—Derry.

IV.

A WEEK'S TOUR FROM DERRY THROUGH DONEGAL.

1st Day, Rail to Stranorlar—Car to Gap of Barnesmore—Lough Esk—Donegal—Killybegs.

2d, Killybegs—Carrick—Excursion to Slieve League and Glen.

3d, Carrick—Glengesh—Glenties—Dungloe.

4th, Dungloe—Gweedore—Excursion to Dunlewy and Errigal.

5th, Gweedore Hotel—Falcarragh—Dunfanaghy—Excursion to Horn Head.

6th, Dunfanaghy — Kilmacrenan — Rathmelton — Fort-Stewart Ferry—Burt—See the Grianan of Aileach—Derry.

V.

A WEEK'S TOUR FROM BELFAST THROUGH DONEGAL.

1st Day, Rail to Strabane and Stranorlar—Car through Gap of Barnesmore to Donegal—Killybegs.

2d, Killybegs—Carrick—Excursion to Slieve League.

3d, Carrick—Glengesh—Ardara—Glenties—Dungloe—Gweedore Hotel.

4th, Gweedore to Dunlewy—Errigal—Lough Beagh (Veagh)—Gartan Lough—Letterkenny.

5th, Letterkenny—Kilmacrenan—Milford—Rathmelton—Excursion to Rathmullan—Climb Croaghin.

6th, Rathmelton—Fort-Stewart Ferry—Burt (see Aileach)—Buncrana—Derry—Belfast.

VI.

ANOTHER ROUTE FROM BELFAST.

1st Day, Rail to Strabane—Car to Letterkenny—See Gartan Lough in the afternoon.

2d, Letterkenny—Kilmacrennan—Dunfunaghy (see Horn Head)—Get on to the Gweedore Hotel.

3d, Gweedore Hotel—Dunlewy—Lough Veagh—Lough Barra—Lough Finn—Glenties.

4th, Glenties—Ardara—Glengesh—Carrick—Ascend Slieve League.

5th, Carrick—Killybegs—Donegal—Ballyshannon.

6th, Ballyshannon (steamer on Lough Erne) to Enniskillen—Rail to Belfast.

INDEX.

Q

DUBLIN: A. MURRAY AND COMPANY, PRINTERS.

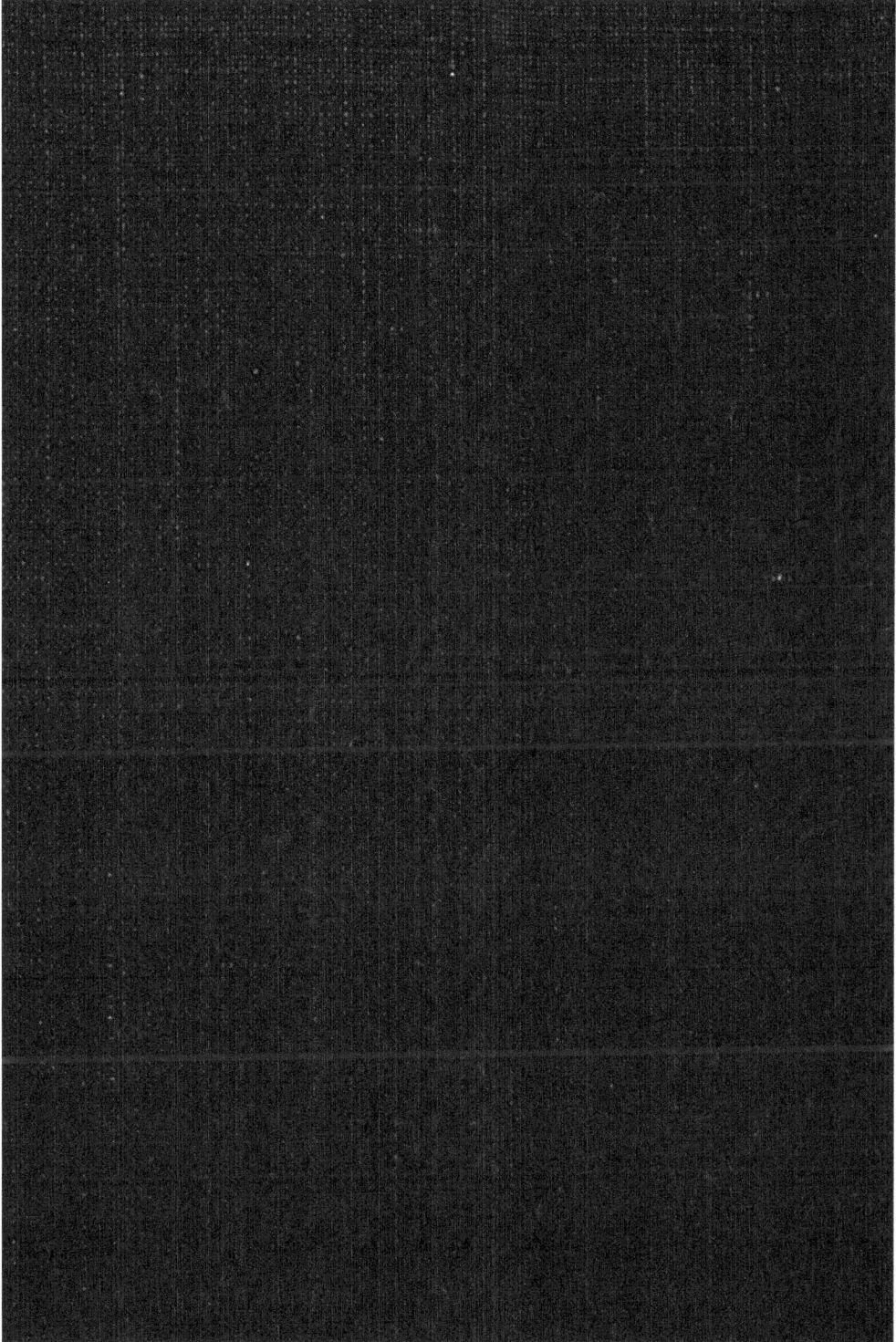

CPSIA information can be obtained
at www.ICGtesting.com
Printed in the USA
BVOW07s1045040416

442856BV00003B/14/P